GW00994557

# FLYING
# WITH THE
# LARKS

## THE EARLY AVIATION
## PIONEERS OF LARK HILL

### TIMOTHY C. BROWN

in association with **National Trust**
Essex County Council

*'A new era in society will commence from the moment that aerial navigation is familiarly realised'*

Sir George Cayley, Aeronautical Experimenter 1773–1857

*This book is dedicated to the aviation pioneers, who lost their lives at Lark Hill and elsewhere, in the furtherance of British aviation, up to and including the outbreak of the First World War in 1914.*

First published 2013
in association with National Trust
by Spellmount, an imprint of

The History Press
The Mill, Brimscombe Port
Stroud, Gloucestershire, GL5 2QG
www.thehistorypress.co.uk

British Library Cataloguing in Publication Data.
A catalogue record for this book is available from the British Library.

ISBN 978 0 7524 8989 6

Typesetting and origination by The History Press
Printed in Great Britain

# CONTENTS

*Appendices*

# PREFACE

As I finish writing this book I cannot help but relate to one of the characters in Proust, who describes a piece he has written as mostly accurate and must surely be of some interest. In the knowledge that many other authors have written informative books on early aviation history in Britain, comprising both the first-hand recollections of people actively involved in this period, and later knowledgeable historical studies; the reader may wonder why I am setting out to compile yet another volume, and what I think I might contribute? The events I will be describing are focused around one location, which seems to have faded in our collective memory when compared to say Farnborough, Brooklands and Hendon; but a location that, in my opinion, plays at least as important a part in the early story as any of those sites. Perhaps my first motivation is that the events I intend to describe occurred around 100 years ago, and as I started this project we were approaching numerous centenaries, which as I write have passed by largely unnoticed.

   I have been fascinated by aviation history since leaving school and joining the Fleet Air Arm. Thirty years later I moved to Wiltshire, and it has been very exciting for me to discover the aviation legacy that surrounds me here; the downside is a profound disappointment that little is being done to preserve that heritage. The knowledge that structures such as the aeroplane sheds at Lark Hill, the balloon sheds at Rollestone Camp, the Royal Flying Corps Officers' Messes at Upavon and Netheravon, and the airfield water tower at Lake Down still exist, provides us all with a tangible link to those early days. But we must not be complacent. Recently, the RFC Officers' Mess at Netheravon and its associated chalets have been closed and are now boarded up, the de Havilland hangars on the airfield there are in a sorry state of repair. As are the RFC hangars at Old Sarum, and the hangars of similar vintage at Yatesbury are scheduled for demolition. Having evidence of the pioneering aviation activities on hand is for many as thrilling as, say, visiting Stonehenge, Wilton House or Salisbury Cathedral. Lark Hill was a key site to the beginnings of aviation in Britain, and I hope you enjoy reading its story and will join me in ensuring we try not to forget about it.

For clarity I have adopted a few language conventions in my text. To preserve accuracy, and a sense of period, I have used original quotations where they are available and these have retained the original spelling and grammar. In English vocabulary there are many words to describe flying machines, and perhaps the one in common-usage today, 'aircraft', is the most generic term. Balloons, gliders, and airships are all 'aircraft' in the broader sense. I prefer 'aeroplane' to the American 'airplane' when describing fixed-wing powered flying machines, and have used 'aircraft' only when a more general term is appropriate. The contemporary spelling 'Lark Hill' is used, except when referring to the present-day Army garrison, as the single-word version 'Larkhill' did not come into common usage until 1919 after the airfield closed. Likewise, 'Hangar' originates from a French word meaning a store, and was not in general use during the period in question, so I use 'shed' which is more chronologically correct. Debate raged at the beginning of the twentieth century over the correct use of the word 'aerodrome'. The American Samuel Langley first coined the term for a flying machine *not* for a field for flying. 'Airfield' has been used throughout, as this seems an entirely appropriate description. Early airfields did not have runways per se, the term 'flying ground' denotes the manoeuvring area where take-offs and landings take place. Finally, I have followed the standard convention of adding the 'RN' suffix to distinguish the naval ranks of Lieutenant and Captain from Army ranks of the same name; and would remind readers that Captain RN is equivalent to Colonel, whilst Lieutenant RN is the equivalent of an Army Captain.

As my reading and research has progressed I have inevitably discovered many discrepancies and variations in the stories told, and unravelling them has been an impossible task. I feel sure there will be passages in my text that some readers will be adamant I have got wrong. My dilemma was that if I used solely corroborated facts it might render the story bland and uninteresting. Wherever possible, details have been checked and either the most reliable, or in my mind logical, version has been used. I realise, of course, that in retelling the story that way I may be creating more controversy, or simply adding to this confusion and apologise if that is indeed the case.

In preparing this account I have drawn on many sources, several of which warrant particular mention. Firstly, *Wings over Wiltshire* by Rod Priddle is a book that describes the history of aviation sites in the county. This monumental piece of research reminded me of stories I thought I had forgotten, and introduced me to many, many more. I can categorically state that reading Rod's book provided me with the inspiration to research further and it was the stepping off point for this work. Next I was led to the Flight Global website. *Flight* magazine has been the leading aviation industry publication for many years, and they are rightly proud of our aviation heritage. Their website makes it possible to view back copies dating from January 1909 (when it was launched as the journal of the Aero Club of the United Kingdom). It is fascinating to be able to read contemporary accounts of key events, and it gave me invaluable access to several rare photographs that have brought this account to life. I am very grateful for the permission from Flight Global to reproduce photographs from this resource. The third source I will single out is Malcolm Hall's book *From Balloon to Box Kite*. This immensely readable account is packed full of accounts and anecdotes, and describes the evolution of military aviation in the Royal Engineers in a level of detail missing in many other books. Finally, Peter Reese's biography of Samuel Cody, *The Flying Cowboy*, is extremely well written and puts the story of Britain's first airman straight.

I must mention my colleagues Ted Mustard and Roger Green. They introduced me to a very knowledgeable local historian, Norman Parker, and the Amesbury Aviation Heritage Centre, and were able to persuade me to join their small National Trust team leading guided walks around the aviation sites surrounding Stonehenge. I am grateful to the author Ray Sangar for his advice and guidance both about the subject and publishing in general, and for access to his own extensive library of books and photographs. My thanks go to Peter Capon, the archivist at the Museum of Army Aviation, Middle Wallop; to Capt. Geoff Bowker RN for his encouragement, and for putting me in touch with Air Cdre Bill Croydon CBE RAF(Retd), a knowledgeable expert on Eastchurch airfield, who previewed my early text and kindly allowed me access to his article on John Dunne. Thanks are due to Jimmy Fuller for permission to use so many of his grandfather's images, to Sir George White, great-grandson of the founder of the Bristol Aeroplane Company, and David Dickson for their support and materials. Thanks also to Prof. Duncan Greenman of the Bristol Airchive for permission to use company photographs in his keeping. Finally thanks to Lucy Evershed at the Stonehenge Landscapes Estate Office and Grant Berry in the National Trust Offices at Swindon for their support and enthusiasm in the early stages that helped get this project off the ground. My wife, Lesley, deserves a mention for the patience she has shown during the hours I have spent in front of my iMac, and her forbearance when I have talked about my 'exciting discoveries' and the odd artefacts I have collected.

I have included a full list of sources and other recommended reading at the end of this book, and made efforts to obtain permission to use copyrighted material. I offer my apologies for any omissions or oversights in this respect, and I ask forbearance in such matters. I would be pleased to give credit, make the necessary acknowledgements and, if so required, delete any material used inappropriately from any future edition.

*Timothy Brown*
*Staverton, 2012*

# INTRODUCTION

Salisbury Plain is a large area of chalk escarpment in southern central England, covering approximately one-tenth of the county of Wiltshire. Within the Plain sits the largest military training area in Britain. Although the British Army is proud of its long history and traditions, its permanent link with the Plain began relatively recently. On 25 March 1897, The War Office[1] completed the purchase of 750 acres of land – on which now sits Bulford Camp – from Miss J. Seymour of East Knoyle, for the sum of £7,500. Over the next five years a further 40,000 acres (approximately 16,000 hectares) were purchased for around £550,000. One hundred years later, the Ministry of Defence owns some 92,000 acres on Salisbury Plain, an area of land equivalent in size to the Isle of Wight and estimated to be worth around £167 million.

Army balloon outside Bristol Flying School shed, c.1912. (J. Fuller)

Training areas will normally accommodate a wide range of activities, and among those conducted on Salisbury Plain from the outset was ballooning. Tethered balloons filled with either hydrogen gas, or sometimes coal gas, were raised as observation platforms for reconnaissance and used to spot the fall of artillery shells. The *Warminster Journal* describes such training, and provides us with one of the earliest references to Lark Hill in the context of aeronautical work when it reported in 1909, 'Experiments in shell firing *at* balloons will begin early this month on Salisbury Plain . . . The 12th Brigade RFA and No.2 Balloon Company RE proceeded to Salisbury Plain from Aldershot . . . in connection with the firing. The Balloon Company will go into camp at Durrington while the howitzer batteries will join the practice camp at Lark Hill . . . '[2]

In fact, at that time the Army had been working with observation balloons for over twenty-five years. The Royal Engineers had opened the Balloon Equipment Store at Woolwich, and began constructing balloons on an experimental basis. Capt. James Lethbridge Brooke Templer, a militia officer serving with The Rifles, was given approval to construct a balloon. Its first flight was over Woolwich on 23 August 1878. Two years later the School of Ballooning had opened at Chatham in Kent. By 1887, Templer was appointed as Instructor in Ballooning on a salary of £600, and had acquired, at personal expense, training grounds near Maidstone. In 1890 the school relocated to Stanhope Lines at Aldershot and was established as a permanent unit. The War Office began to deploy balloon sections to conflicts in Bechuanaland (now Botswana) and Sudan during the latter part of the nineteenth century, but these forays were poorly funded and ineffective. The second Boer War proved to be a turning point. Thirty balloons that were sent to South Africa in 1899 were well utilised. A first-hand account written by John Lane, a Boer soldier on the receiving end, gives clear evidence of the effectiveness of balloon observation and the demoralizing effect they could have. Lane writes of how, on sighting a British balloon over their positions, 'Some follows shouted to me to hide away . . . it does not matter now, its all up, they will be able to find out every hole we are in and will pour in a hell of shells.'[3] A balloon section was present at the siege of Ladysmith, continuing operations until it ran out of gas.

The problem with gas-filled balloons was they could only be launched, and operate, in the lightest winds. The solution was thought to lie in airships and man-lifting kites, the latter actually thriving in stronger wind conditions; however, it was the development of another type of aircraft at the start of the twentieth century, the powered aeroplane, that would put a rather isolated corner of Salisbury Plain, known by locals as The Hill of Larks, onto the map.

Throughout the nineteenth century, various experimenters strived to achieve man's long-held ambition to fly. It will be well known that in 1903, whilst the War Office was acquiring land on Salisbury Plain, Wilbur and Orville Wright, two bicycle makers from Ohio, and their oft forgotten mechanic Charles Turner, were getting closer to building a successful powered flying machine. The brothers had been fascinated by flight since childhood when, one day in the 1870s, their father brought home a flying toy helicopter. And it was around 1898 or 1899 that they began conducting serious research and experiments with gliders, hoping, in due course, to be able to fit one with a small engine and so enjoy unrestricted flight. They designed and built their own 8hp motor, which drove a propeller they had had made in their workshop beside their home in Dayton. Based on the recommendation of their friend, fellow experimenter and confident Octavus Chanute[4], they chose to conduct their experiments in North Carolina, where they were advised they could expect strong and constant winds. When they wrote to the Postmaster on the small island of Kitty Hawk, enquiring whether it was a suitable area, he confirmed that, 'The sand hills were round and soft, well fitted for boys playing with flying machines.'[5]

The Wright brothers' work culminated there on 17 December 1903, where from sand dunes beside the Atlantic ocean known as Kill Devil Hills, Orville took off at 10.35 a.m in a machine the brothers termed a powered flyer, but which the *Daily Mail* naively announced to its British readership as a 'balloonless airship'. That first flight lasted only twelve seconds, and covered a distance less than the wingspan of a Boeing 747 airliner. However, by the end of the day the brothers had each flown twice, and on one occasion had been airborne for almost a minute and flown a distance of around 850ft. Their last flight was made in testing winds of around 25kts but, unfortunately, like so many early flights, ended with a heavy landing that damaged their flyer. Nevertheless, their work that day entered the record books, and so began a chain of work and further development that would

No.3 Sqn RFC Bristol Prier-Dickson monoplane at Lark Hill, c.1912. (J. Fuller)

shape mankind's progress through the twentieth century, and ultimately affect the lives of every person who would live on the planet in some way or another.

Today, in Wiltshire, a few hundred yards south of an unclassified road known as The Packway, that runs between the villages of Durrington and Shrewton, stand five large corrugated iron sheds (Grid Reference: SU144437). Currently used to store surplus Army furniture, these listed structures, and a small stone memorial nearby, are the only visible evidence marking the site of Lark Hill airfield. This airfield had a short life from 1909-14, and in that time it was used by both military and civilian aviators. But by 1913, when the Royal Flying Corps was just one year old, most of the military activities had relocated elsewhere, and before the start of the Great War the airfield closed altogether. In the five years it had been in existence, Lark Hill was the location of one of the first flying schools in Britain, where many aviation pioneers learnt to fly, and the site where important trial and development work was undertaken. It lays claim to being Britain's first military airfield and was also home to the first British military fixed-wing aeroplane squadron.

# 1

# SOARING LIKE AN EAGLE

In 1903, news of the Wright brothers' successful flight broke slowly. It is believed that the first report came via a telegraph operator who had intercepted a message the brothers sent to their father telling of their achievement. The message read, 'Success four flights Thursday morning started from level with engine power alone . . . inform press . . . home Christmas'.[1] The story reached a local newspaper, appropriately called the *Virginian Pilot*, on 18 December 1903, and they published a small news item that was picked up the following day by *The Washington Post*, under the somewhat extravagant headline 'Soaring Like an Eagle'.

With hindsight, one might imagine the news of the first successful powered flight would be a massive scoop, however, at the time it almost passed by a sceptical public unnoticed. Many simply refused to believe the story, claiming flight was impossible or that it was a hoax; there were many more whom, whilst accepting the possibility of flight, saw it as mere folly and saw no value in its pursuance. Field Marshal Sir W.G. Nicholson, a British Army officer (who would become Chief of the Imperial General Staff 1909-12), was one of the latter school. An outspoken gentleman, he is said to have once proclaimed, 'Aviation is a useless and expensive fad advocated by a few individuals whose ideas are unworthy of attention',[2] and Nicholson remained convinced that aeroplanes would be worthless as means of scouting, as it would surely be impossible to accurately observe activity on the ground whilst travelling at 'high speed' through the air. Nicholson's statement, like others who later rejected the personal computer, and the decision not to sign up The Beatles, has gone down in history as profoundly wrong. Nevertheless, among those who shared his belief was the then editor of *The Times Engineering Supplement*. When Alliott V. Roe[3] wrote to the paper in February 1906 his letter was dismissed as a cheap attempt to publicise Roe's fanciful aeronautical experiments. Some months later the paper deigned to print Roe's letter, but famously added the following caution; 'All attempts at artificial aviation are . . . dangerous to human life (and) foredoomed to failure from the engineering standpoint.'[4]

Lt Col John Capper and
Katherine Wright. (*Flight*)

Thankfully not everyone had such negative views. John Capper was a Lieutenant Colonel in the Royal Engineers. Capper was fascinated by the potential of heavier-than-air flying machines, and although he was once given the nickname 'Stone-age' by junior officers for his Luddite tendencies, this comment on his personality now appears quite undeserved. He had first experienced ballooning whilst training on Salisbury Plain, and in May 1906 was appointed Commandant of the Balloon School at Farnborough. In this role he would play a significant part in the start of aviation in Britain. Shortly after taking up that post he was invited to speak at the Royal United Services Institute where he told his audience: 'In a few years we may expect to see men moving swiftly through the air on simple surfaces just as a gliding bird moves . . .' [5]

Capper's involvement with aeroplanes began when he was asked by his commanding officer, now Col James Templer, to visit the St Louis Universal Exposition, or World's Fair, in October 1904. The fair would include an International Aeronautical Congress, so Templer asked Capper to go along and see if there was anything of interest. Aware of the Wright brothers' achievement, and realising this was an opportunity not to be missed, Capper obtained a letter of introduction to them from a mutual friend, Patrick Alexander, before he set sail for America with his wife Edith. Whilst Capper's subsequent dealings with the Wright brothers have no direct relevance to the Lark Hill story, the difficult negotiations that follow over the next few years sets the scene for early aviation development in Europe, and, therefore, is an appropriate starting point of our story.

Britain was a world leader in balloon technology, so unsurprisingly Capper found little of interest in St Louis. He took leave with Edith for Ohio, where they received a congenial welcome from the Wright family. John and Edith got on remarkably well with Wilbur and Orville, their sister Katharine and father Milton, and they immediately became good friends. The Cappers were invited to stay with the Wrights at their home in Hawthorn Street, Dayton, where the brothers engaged John, exhaustively talking about their experiments.

They allowed him to read eyewitness accounts of their flights and showed him photographs of the flyer airborne. Capper could not fail to be impressed, later describing the brothers as well-educated men and capable mechanics; he did not for a moment think it strange he had not been shown the actual machine, as he was told it had been dismantled and was in storage.

Several sources claim that during this visit the Wrights made Capper an offer to work solely for the British Government, however, in his book *Miracle at Kitty Hawk: The Letters of Wilbur & Orville Wright*, Fred C. Kelly confirms it was Capper who made the approach, asking the brothers to make his government some kind of proposal. Orville had already described their first flights as, 'very modest compared with that of birds'[6] and he and his brother realised there was still a lot of work to do and improvements to make before their flyer was commercially viable, so they informed Capper they were not yet ready to talk business. The brothers set to work improving their machine, refining their piloting skills, and increased the flight distance and duration markedly. In January 1905 the brothers wrote to Capper saying, 'We are ready to enter into a contract with the British Government to construct and deliver to it an aerial scouting machine of the aeroplane type . . .' they added, 'if you think it probable that an offer . . . would receive consideration from your Government at this time, we will be glad to give further consideration to matters of detail.'[7] This approach has been wrongly interpreted as an offer to deal solely with the British Government. Nine days after posting their letter to Capper, and timed carefully so as to arrive at precisely the same time, the Wrights wrote to the U.S. Government. The letter said:

During the year 1904, one hundred and five flights were made at our experimenting station, on the Huffman prairie, east of the city; and though our experience in handling the machine has been too short to give any high degree of skill, we nevertheless succeeded, toward the end of the season, in making two flights of five minutes each, in which we sailed round and round the field until a distance of about three miles had been covered. The numerous flights have made it quite certain that flying has been brought to a point where it can be made of great practical use in various ways, one of which is that of scouting and carrying messages in time of war. If the latter features are of interest to our own government, we shall be pleased to take up the matter either on a basis of providing machines of agreed specification, at a contract price, or of furnishing all the scientific and practical information we have accumulated in these years of experimenting . . . [8]

The Wright brothers had previously discussed making such an offer with their Congressman, Robert M. Nevin, and he had in turn agreed to personally recommend their proposal to the War Department. Unfortunately, Nevin was ill when the brothers' letter arrived and his staff passed it directly to the Secretary of War, Congressman William H. Taft. He mistook this apparently unsolicited approach as a request for funding for experiments, and sent back a stock letter of rejection, not once but twice. The rebuff shocked the brothers, and when they were discussing it with Chanute he offered to take up the matter with President Jefferson, who he knew personally. But, on 1 June 1905, Wilbur informed Chanute, 'It is no pleasant thought that any foreign country should take from America any share of the glory of having conquered the flying problem… it has been for years our business practice to sell goods to those who wished to buy, instead of trying to force goods upon people who did not want them. If the American government has decided to spend no money on flying machines… we are sorry, but we cannot reasonably object. They are the judges.'[9] Their letter to Britain had indeed been more enthusiastically received. Capper had shown it to his superiors at Aldershot, who in turn passed it swiftly onto the Army Council in Whitehall. They proposed that Col Hubert J. Foster, the British Military Attaché in Washington, should visit the brothers and observe a flight. The council wrote back to the Wright brothers, requesting they make a definitive offer, and instructed Foster to make the necessary arrangements. But the letter to Foster arrived when he was away from his desk on duty in Mexico, and he did not receive it until some months later. When he eventually spoke to Wilbur on 18 November 1905 he learnt that the brothers were not prepared to demonstrate their machine, or even allow anyone to set eyes upon it, until the British Government had signed a binding contractual agreement.

On first encounter this seems an unlikely demand, and many have been puzzled by Wilbur's intransigence. The brothers have been accused of not wanting to sell their invention and in the process holding back aviation development for years. Undoubtedly, Wilbur and Orville were guarded, and it might be said that they were protective, but they were not secretive. They invited the local communities to come out and witness their flights; they even welcomed newspaper reporters to attend on the understanding that no photographs were taken. They did insist any written reports should not be sensationalist, but this was a safety precaution

Wilbur and Orville Wright
preparing for a flight. (*Flight*)

to avoid attracting overlarge crowds, rather than a reluctance to show their work. This suggests that the men knew the value of their invention, but fully realised other ambitious aviators would be quite willing to steal their ideas. Indeed, their own government had previously shown, on several occasions, a willingness to purloin any innovative design, leaving the rightful owner no recourse other than legal action – a lengthy and costly process that the brothers knew they could not afford. They had applied for a patent for their invention on 23 March 1903, but two years later it had still not been granted. In fact, U.S. Patent No. 821393 was not issued until 22 May 1906, and then, owing to an oversight in their original application, it covered the system for operating the control surfaces of their flyer rather than the whole aeroplane and so gave little overall protection to their invention. When the reader learns that, despite their reticence, the brothers would subsequently enter into at least eleven legal actions for patent infringements, the cautious attitude they maintained towards their work may be better understood?

Unable to advise under precisely what terms they might sell a machine to the War Office, Wilbur and Orville suggested they would stage a demonstration and set their fee on the basis of £50 per mile flown. In Britain, there were rumours the brothers were preparing their machine for a 500-mile flight, and so it was assumed the final price might be as much as £25,000. Although this distance would have been a reasonable goal to demonstrate the viability of their flyer, the truth is the brothers were some way from achieving it at that time. Of the many flights they conducted in 1904 their longest was just five minutes and four seconds, and although improvements were being made during 1905, the best flight they achieved that year was still only thirty-eight minutes in duration and covered just 24 miles – a long way short of the alleged goal. However, the detractors continued to press the point, along with their view that a British aeroplane could be built for a fraction of the 'assumed' cost. So, in February 1906, without a firm offer being put on the table, the Director of Artillery, Colonel Charles Hadden, wrote to the brothers rejecting their proposal. Undaunted, Wilbur and Orville contacted the governments of Germany, Italy, Russia, Austria, France and Japan, before writing again to Britain in May 1906. This second approach resulted in a meeting with Foster's replacement, Colonel Albert E. Gleichen the following August. The brothers answered Gleichen's questions frankly and suggested they would be willing to sell the British Government an aeroplane for 100,000 dollars, plus a similar amount for their services, scientific knowledge and experimental results, and would continue to work for a further four years (the sum expected was around £40,000 at the prevailing rate of exchange). Upon hearing this, their compatriot Chanute commented that he thought their price was very high. Gliechen submitted his report to the War Office, who in turn passed it onto Capper, with the following comment, 'The accompanying letters from the Wright Cycle Co. Ltd, and the military attaché Washington, are forwarded for your remarks, but there appears to be no probability of approval being given for the expenditure of the large sum asked for.'[10] Considering the enthusiasm he had once shown, Capper's response was surprising; 'There appears to be little doubt that the machine has done all the brothers claim for it . . . (but) I cannot think that a machine so limited in capacity can have great practical value except as leading to the building of better ones and therefore the purchase would be of no great assistance to us.'[11] It is, however, worth noting these decisions were being made against the background of a Liberal Government who had just defeated the Conservatives in the December 1905 General Election, with a manifesto promising to exercise strict economy in the field of defence expenditure.

As well as their dealings with the War Office, the Wright brothers had approached the Admiralty in the hope that the Royal Navy might also be interested in procuring a flyer. However, having consulted with his expert advisors Lord Tweedmouth, the First Sea Lord, wrote back thanking the brothers for their proposal, but saying that the Admiralty Board had, after careful consideration, arrived at the conclusion that their aeroplane would not be of any practical use to the Royal Navy. The Wright brothers became distracted by all these negotiations and stopped all experimentation. They did no flying from 1906 until they had negotiated an agreement with the French Government and staged flying demonstrations with their Wright Model A Flyer, a development of their original machine, during the summer of 1908.

# 2

## SECOND TO NONE

Capper's loss of confidence in Wilbur and Orville might be explained by another reason. Since 1905 he had become deeply involved in aviation experiments in Britain and had gone on record as saying, 'We must do our utmost to build successful machines ourselves and learn their use'[1]; a proposal that would undoubtedly enhance the international reputation of the Balloon Factory and British aviation in general. In 1903, Capper had met a larger than life character by the name of Samuel Franklin Cowdery (aka Samuel 'Colonel' Cody). Cody first came to Britain several years earlier to sell horses to the Army. He met and fell in love with his agent's married daughter, Lela. Cody returned to Britain several times, before persuading his wife Maud to travel with him and set up home permanently here. Cody was now styling himself on William 'Buffalo Bill' Cody; he had adopted the surname and established a spectacular touring show, in which he demonstrated his sharp-shooting skills and horsemanship, whilst Lela would be hoisted hundreds of feet above the audience in a basket suspended from a string of kites.

Samuel F. Cody. (*Flight*)

The first reference to Cody's kite flying was a record of a demonstration he staged at Houghton House, Carlisle in April 1899, which was reported in the local press. It is stated, 'He flew kites of immense size and square shaped, sent up in tandem fashion one after another on strong steel piano wire. The third or fourth kite had a seat slung from it in which a man sat.'[2] In 1901 Cody contacted the War Office offering to demonstrate the military potential of his kites. He was not completely unknown to them, having written to them during the Boer war, offering to train snipers for the British Army, but this proposal was rejected as he was not a British subject. In this second approach, Cody wrote, 'I believe I possess certain secrets which could be of use to the government in the way of kite flying.'[3] However, the letter appears to have remained in the army's pending files. On 5 September 1902 Cody set a kite altitude record of 14,000ft, and, after competing in the International Kite Trials near Worthing, was elected a member of the Aeronautical Society of Great Britain. Another gentleman similarly honoured and attending the same enrolment ceremony, was Col Capper. This was the first time the two men had met.

Ever the experimenter, Cody completed a crossing of the English Channel in a canoe towed by a kite on 6 November 1903, and asked to demonstrate a 'man-lifter' kite to the Royal Navy. The trials were held at HMS *Excellent* on Whale Island, Portsmouth, but despite being impressed the Admiralty was hesitant. It did, however, suggest to the War Office that the kites might have military value, and shortly afterwards Cody was invited to the Balloon Factory at Farnborough.[4] This demonstration was witnessed by Capper, who wrote, 'I recommend that one set of man-lifting and one set of signal kites be purchased from Mr Cody . . .

Officers of the Balloon Factory 1907. Front row: Lt John Dunne, Lt Col Capper and Samuel Cody. (Unknown)

[he] is perhaps the greatest living expert in the art of kite flying [and] should be employed as an Instructor for at least three months.'[5] Capper's recommendation was accepted and the War Office appointed Cody as the Chief Kite Instructor on a salary of £50 a month in the spring of 1905.[6] In accepting this position, Cody had to give up his Klondyke Nugget shows and the quite lucrative theatre appearances. He was also required to surrender the patent for his kites, although it would be more than seven years before he received payment for these, and only then by recourse of the law courts.

Despite this, Cody enjoyed working with Capper and the resources that were made available to him at Farnborough. He shared the colonel's dream of powered flight, and was working along similar lines to the Wright brothers i.e. a belief that the secret to successful powered flight was to have first mastered proper control of the glider. Cody's experiments went well. Army personnel were soon airborne in kites that, on reaching an appropriate height, were released from their cables so the pilot could glide freely back to the ground. In 1906 Cody stated, 'I do not wish to assert that I have produced a flying machine in the full sense but . . . I hope at no distant date to play an important part in the complete conquest of the air.'[7] All he needed now was a suitably powerful, but lightweight, engine.

It should not be surprising to learn that Cody, as an employee at the Balloon Factory, had also been working on an airship known as British Army Airship No.1. Capper had initiated this project with the intention of staging an attention-grabbing flight in response to the news that the former German general, Count Zeppelin, was building and flying dirigibles (airships) over Lake Constance. Cody had been drafted in to help. He stopped his aeroplane experiments and, with funding from The Royal Engineers' Committee, travelled to Paris where he bought a small marine engine from the Antoinette Company for £550. This was brought back to Farnborough and fitted to the airship they were constructing, which had been given the name *Nulli Secundus* (Second to None) by HRH King Edward VII. Having spent the morning of 5 October 1907 ensuring they were ready for flight, the airship took off at 11.00 a.m., their destination was London, 40 miles away. Cody sounded a klaxon as they approached the outskirts of the city, lest anyone failed to notice the large airship cruising at a speed of around 25kts at a height of 800ft above the ground. They literally did 'stop traffic' in the capital for about half an hour. After passing the Crystal Palace and Hyde Park, the airship flew low over Buckingham Palace and onto Whitehall, where they saluted notable members of the Army Council who had gathered on the roof of the War Office, before heading east towards St Paul's Cathedral, which they orbited several times. But when they turned for home, high winds slowed their progress and the crew decided to land on the cycle track near Crystal Palace. The airship remained there for a few days when, on the grounds of safety, it was decided to dismantle it and return it to Farnborough by road. In the process of dismantling, its precious and delicate 'goldbeaters skin' gas envelopes were irreparably damaged.

The airship *Nulli Secundus* orbits St Paul's Cathedral, 5 October 1907. (Author's collection)

The Army Council was informed of Cody's aeroplane work and, perhaps buoyed by his part in the successful airship demonstration, agreed to award some funds towards the construction of an aeroplane that should be known as British Army Aeroplane No.1. Although this funding amounted to only £50, someone with Cody's degree of determination was not going to be put off by something as simple as a lack of money. He seized the opportunity and removed the engine from the airship and planned to fit it to one of his gliders. But Capper was determined to improve the airship concept and began to draw up plans for *Nulli Secundus II* (the irony of choosing this name apparently escaped them), so Cody was asked to surrender the Antoinette engine and his work came to a temporary halt.

The work of another junior Army officer had also been attracting interest at Farnborough. Lieut John William Dunne of the Royal Wiltshire Regiment had been experimenting with model gliders and helicopters. He was very friendly with the author H.G. Wells and had provided drawings for Wells' book *War in the*

*Air* that described a future, devastating aerial conflict; and in return the author based a character in the book on the young army officer. Whilst serving with the Mounted Infantry in South Africa, Dunne had contracted typhoid that left him with a heart condition and he had been sent back to Britain in 1902. Learning of the Wright brothers' success the following year, Dunne noted that reports said their Flyer was a very difficult machine to control.[8] He felt that in order for such a machine to be useful for military purposes it should be stable and very easy to fly, so that the pilot was not compelled to give all his attention to the controls and could undertake other tasks. His father, General Sir John Harte Dunne KCB, was a man with influential friends and contacts, who also believed in the potential of aeroplanes. Gen. Dunne passed on a written account of his son's work to the Chairman of the Council of the Aeronautical Society, Maj. Baden Baden-Powell (brother of the founder of the Boy Scout movement). Dunne's essay was an impressive piece of work and with it he gained access into the 'right circles' to further promote his ideas. When a representative from the War Office saw several of Dunne's model aircraft, word of this work reached the Balloon Factory. Capper arranged to meet with Dunne. They got on well, Capper finding he had more in common with the gentleman son of a retired General than with Cody the showman. Capper wrote to Baden-Powell: 'I think Dunne should be a useful man; he seems to have a very thorough idea of the theory of gliders, and to have arrived at what, in small models, is a perfectly stable machine. I hope we shall be permitted to make use of his services.'[9]

Lt John Dunne. (*Flight*)

When Capper became superintendent of the Balloon Factory he was impatient to have Dunne on his team, and wrote discreetly, 'We are wasting an awful lot of time waiting for official sanction . . . If you do not mind working quietly and saying nothing about it, it would be just as well for you to come down immediately.'[10] In public, at least, Capper was wise enough to hedge his bets, saying that one of these two men 'Seems likely to lead us in the same direction as Messrs Wrights' developments . . .'[11] Dunne started work at Farnborough on 7 June 1906 whereupon he was paid half a guinea a day when in attendance.[12]

Capper had arranged that the construction work would be split around various workshops. The aim being that no individual, other than Dunne and his trusted sixteen-year-old assistant, Percy Gurr, would gain detailed knowledge of their V-shaped, tail-less glider known simply as D1. Gurr later recalled climbing high into the rafters of an empty balloon shed where small paper scale-models were dropped from the girders, a careful record being kept of the length of glide and performance of each. As the design was perfected, they built larger versions. Eventually a 3ft wingspan model was constructed from umbrella tubing with wings covered with Japanese silk. It was carefully packed into a cardboard box and taken by hansom cab to a patch of heath land about 5 miles from Farnborough, where the cabbie was given strict instructions to wait at the foot of a hill known as Caesar's Camp, whilst Dunne and Gurr climbed to the top to conduct their tests. The model performed well, and encouraged by this Dunne set about building a full-sized version of his glider, which would be ready to trial the following year.

And so, whilst Cody was being kept occupied working on the airship, Dunne was urged to press ahead with his work on his aeroplane. In order to preserve the project's secrecy, Capper sought permission from the Marquis of Tullibardine to conduct the trials on his family's property at Blair Atholl in Scotland. Capper and Dunne had both served with Tullibardine during the Boer War, and he was perfectly happy to assist. The chosen site, a grouse moor overlooking Glen Tilt, provided a discrete venue away from the public gaze. A company of Royal Engineers were dispatched from Farnborough, with instructions to travel in plain clothing to avoid drawing attention to themselves. On arrival, the Sappers under the command of Lieut Francis Westland, joined forces with the men of the Duke's private army[13] and assisted by keeping away unwanted onlookers. The Duke had put out word that local people were to stay indoors and keep their curtains drawn, 'lest they catch a glance of the machine', and what the Duke wanted, the Duke got.

His doctor had forbidden Dunne to fly except when absolutely necessary to check the balance of his aeroplane, so he sought help from Capper and Tullibardine who both flew the D1 glider. Neither were particularly experienced pilots and, on one occasion, as the Marquis was about to launch, he was alarmed to see the doctor laying out his medical equipment on a white sheet at the foot of the hill. Capper conducted the final test, and for his protection he wore a fencing facemask. The flight was a brief one, ending in a collision with a dry stonewall;

fortunately, Capper's only injury was a small cut to his face. The project's reputation might not have got off so lightly, for the two senior officers responsible for controlling Farnborough's aeronautical activities, Major General Sir Charles Hadden (Master-General of Ordnance) and Brigadier General Sir Richard Ruck (Director of Fortifications and Works), were among the dignitaries who had been invited to witness the attempt. They could not have been very impressed.

Whilst the airframe of D1 was being repaired, various engines were tried in preparation for an attempt at powered flight; these included fitting two small Buchet engines, and a single REP unit driving two propellers through gears and chains, onto the wing. Both arrangements proved very inefficient, and the combined power output was estimated at just 12hp. Nevertheless, they agreed they would have another attempt at flight. The aeroplane was loaded onto a wheeled trolley, positioned at the top of a track of wooden planks laid down the hillside to reduce friction during the take-off run, and they were ready. The security measures had inevitably attracted the curious and, on 26 September 1907, having ignored requests to pay no attention to the experiments, a reporter from the *Daily Express* managed to sneak past the guards and take up a position a discrete distance away from which he could observe the activities on the hill known as 'Meail Dail-mm'. He later described what he saw; 'The machine, a lightly built, delicately framed structure, was brought out from its shed shortly before midday. In general appearance, as seen through a pair of powerful field glasses, it is like a large butterfly, with wings always extended, and an airiness that would seen unequal to the result it was expected to achieve.' Dunne's first attempt at powered flight was reported as follows, 'The engineers who are in charge of the station ran the machine for some distance on attached wheels, but before the aeroplane rose into the air a gust of wind blowing heavily down the valley

Dunne D1 Glider at Blair Atholl, 1907. (Unknown)

swept by, and the ropes by which the machine was held were not released.' The wind did not abate and the trial was cancelled. Our journalist noted he was not the only unwelcome onlooker. 'Two agents of a foreign Government actually penetrated the mountain fastnesses'. They were observed behind a ridge, which commands the aeroplane shed, to which they had crept under cover of Scotch mist. The Marquis of Tullibardine's scouts saw them, and made rapidly up the slope. The foreigners retreated, and left behind them a telescopic lens, field glasses and cameras. A few days later another attempt at flight was made, witnessed by the Secretary of War, Lord Haldane, who happened to be travelling in the area; but this was no more successful than the previous attempts, and 'the trolley ran straight off the track and slid the machine onto its nose.' The experiments were brought to a halt and D1 was taken back to Farnborough. Capper's report on the proceedings was nothing but optimistic, perhaps in an attempt to justify the work and secure continued support. He said, 'The result, to an unskilled eye merely disastrous, in effect showed that Lieutenant Dunne's calculations and experiments were entirely correct, the machine remaining airborne during a period of eight seconds.' Somehow this worked, and Capper managed to persuade Haldane that another round of experiments should be conducted.

But it was September 1908 before two new machines were ready to resume the trial. Two experienced balloon pilots, the Assistant Supervisor at the Balloon Factory, Capt. Alan Carden RE, and Lancelot Gibbs, a Lieutenant in the militia, travelled to Blair Atholl to assist Dunne. Gibbs managed several successful flights in the D3 glider, but was unable to achieve anything more than a short 157ft hop in the powered D4 aeroplane. Back at Farnborough, Cody had also managed to fly very short distances, but unlike the Blair Atholl trials, the Balloon Factory had been keeping the newspapers informed of progress. (It has been suggested this may have even been part of a tacit agreement for them not drawing attention to Dunne's work in Scotland?) Anxious to report a successful flight the journalists quickly bored of Cody's largely earth-bound excursions and impatiently demanded to know, 'Why he didn't get into the air like the Wrights and the French pilots?' Capper explained that the machine was simply not yet ready to fly, and that Cody was following instructions, but this failed to satisfy them and the criticisms continued to flood in. Cody was oblivious to this and pressed on with his work. Gibbs' flight in Scotland, achieved on 16 May 1908, was the first ever-recorded powered flight in Britain, when he covered a distance of just 40ft. But the RAeC (Royal Aero Club of the United Kingdom) had decreed that in order to qualify as a 'first flight' the trip should be sustained and cover a distance of more than a quarter of a mile, so they discounted both these flights.

Cody was asked to surrender the Antoinette engine, which would have been a major setback, except that as luck would have it, the War Office had gone on to purchase a second engine as a spare. It had now arrived at Farnborough and was possibly a better motor than the original, and Cody was granted access.

Determined to succeed, he built a wind tunnel from the large fan that had been used to inflate *Nulli Secundis* to test his design, and as a result rebuilt most of its wings. With these modifications complete, British Army Aeroplane No.1, a contraption built of hickory, bamboo and cloth-covered wings 'doped' with starch extracted from tapioca and powered by a motorboat engine, was ready. It was moved to a large expanse of common land near Aldershot, known as Laffan's Plain, and there made another short and uncontrolled flight on 29 September. Further adjustments were made and then, with Capper's approval, the gates were opened and members of the press invited to Laffen's Plain on 13 October 1908. Despite witnessing three very short flights the press were disappointed; the journalist from *The Times* reporting, 'The machine showed no disposition to rise.'

Three days later, and still undeterred, Cody was preparing for another day of testing. In a surge of optimism he attached a Union flag to a rear boom of his aeroplane before pushing it out from the shed. Whilst conducting some fast taxiing checks, Cody noted the machine skipped off the ground, and on reaching the top of the hill, he navigated around a clump of trees and set off down the slope at speed. Despite running downwind, the aeroplane leapt into the air and rose steadily to a height of 20-30ft. Seeing two groups of trees ahead, Cody climbed and overflew the first but was unsure he could repeat this with the second, taller clump and decided to land on a level area of grass beside it. But, in trying to turn, he applied the rudder crudely and the aeroplane sideslipped; its wing tip touched the ground and the machine crashed, an event described optimistically in some sources as a 'heavy landing'. The pilot escaped with a cut to his forehead.

In a later report, Capper wrote, 'The damage done to the machine is: left wing, good deal broken up, silk somewhat torn, head rudder stays damaged, right wing slightly damaged, wheels buckled, engine fly-wheel broken.'[14] Cody had been airborne for less than a minute but had crucially covered a distance of 1390ft (424m), and therefore his flight, on 16 October 1908, entered into the record books as the first sustained powered flight in Britain in a heavier-than-air machine. It was less than one month after the first Ford Model T mass-produced car had driven off the production line in Detroit.

Unfortunately, the few dogged reporters who witnessed the event were more interested in reporting the crash than the flight itself; and several of their colleagues, others who had departed early, complained to Capper that they had not been informed that a flight attempt was going to be made. Capper had not only lost patience with the media, but was reportedly furious he had not had the chance to invite his superiors to witness the flight. He dodged the reporters' protests claiming, with some honesty, it was not the intention to fly that day and that Cody had been caught by an unexpected gust of wind. Cody, on the other hand, was somewhat more truthful. He blamed the crash on his lack of skill and inexperience. However, accomplished or not, Dunne and Cody's flights had been, the seed had been sown and the story of aviation in Britain had begun.

Cody's British Army Aeroplane No.1 flies at Laffen's Plain, 16 October 1908. (War Department)

As has been previously suggested, it is thought Capper's superiors were not too impressed with the various attempts. The historian Penrose writes, 'It was bad enough that Capper piloted Dunne's glider straight into a stone wall before the assembled War Office dignitaries the year before ... now an illiterate cowboy had piloted his own untried aircraft virtually headlong into a clump of trees.'[15]  From the meagre £50 budget originally allocated to Cody, expenditure on his and Dunne's machines had now exceeded £2,500 (the lion's share of this having been spent on the latter project). The Committee for Imperial Defence met just one week after Cody's flight and formed a sub-committee under the chairmanship of Lord Esher. Comprising David-Lloyd George MP (Chancellor of the Exchequer), Richard Haldane (Secretary of State for War), Reginald McKenna (First Lord of the Admiralty), Admiral Sir Charles Ottley (Secretary) and Capt. Reginald Bacon RN. However, three senior army officers dominated the group – the aeroplane despising General Sir William Nicholson (Chief of the General Staff), Maj. Gen. John Ewart (Director of Military Operations) and Maj. Gen. Sir Charles Hadden (Master General of the Ordnance).

A powerful committee, but in truth, one in which the members were either inexperienced in the posts they occupied or held extremely biased viewpoints. Ewart and Hadden were deferential to the opinion of their superior officer Nicholson. The sub-committee met four times, during which they heard evidence from the balloonists, the Honourable Charles Rolls and Maj. B.F.S. Baden-Powell, as well as Col Capper and Sir Hiram Maxim. The latter, an elderly semi-retired industrialist, who had conducted some early aeronautical experiments himself, declared, 'I am familiar with everything done on the planet regarding flying machines', and against

this arrogance everyone else's evidence took
second place.

When Esher presented the sub-
committee's conclusions, in the
form of an 80,000 word report, they
recommended to the CID that 'Aviation
pose(s) no threat to Britain, nor (does
it) promise any advantages'.[16] The Prime
Minister, Herbert Asquith, decided no
more funds would be made available for
powered-flight experiments, and the War
Office was informed that Government policy
was henceforth: 'Advantage should be taken of
private enterprise' – i.e. it was to rely on the private
experiments being conducted by military personnel and other pioneers. Perhaps in
adopting this stance Asquith was fully aware of the potential political embarrassment,
and that by avoiding the inherent risks was unlikely to be exposed to any further
humiliation in the media? The balloon and airship lobby, however, did not fair too
badly, and £10,000 was allocated to the Army's balloon units, whilst the Naval
Estimates included £35,000 for the construction of a non-dirigible airship. His
Majesty's Airship No.1 was ironically nicknamed 'Mayfly'. It was commissioned
by Vickers, but was written off by a gust of wind whilst being taken from its shed
before its maiden flight, at Barrow-in-Furness in 1911.

It was left to Capper to tell his colleagues Dunne and Cody their services were
no longer required at the Balloon Factory. Cody had a powerful ally in the form
of Gen. Sir Smith-Dorrien (Commander-in-Chief at Aldershot) who, despite
resistance from the War Office, gave permission for Cody and his team to use
the Balloon Factory sheds until they had constructed their own on nearby land
on the banks of the Basingstoke Canal. He also arranged for him to continue to
have use of one of the Factory's Antoinette engines. With that, Cody rebuilt the
aeroplane at his own expense, and it flew again in various forms.

Dunne formed a business consortium with Tullibardine and others, known
as the Blair Atholl Aeroplane Syndicate, that continued to develop his stable
aeroplane concept. Whilst shopping in London one day, Dunne saw some model
aeroplanes in the window of Gamages department store in Holborn that were
very similar to his own design. He entered the store and asked to speak to the
manager, who told him the models had been built by a twenty-three-year-old
electrical engineer named Richard Fairey, who was working at Finchley Power

The Marquis of Tullibardine. (*Flight*)

Station. Dunne arranged to meet Fairey and learnt that he had recently won first prize in a flying model competition at Crystal Palace. Dunne had heard enough, and asked him to become his General Manager.[17]

The stability of Dunne's designs was unquestionable. In 1910, one flew for more than 2 miles, during which the pilot had only to touch the controls for take-off and landing. Capt. Alan Carden RE bought Dunne's D8 and flew it on many occasions, despite only having one arm, and during a demonstration in 1913 the French pilot Félix, flying the machine solo, climbed out of the cockpit and stood on the wing. The stable aeroplane was indeed an ideal observation and scouting platform, but that stability came at a price. The machines were difficult to manoeuvre and, therefore, could not evade aggressive, agile fighter aircraft. A threat, despite his obvious imagination, Dunne had not foreseen.

Britain had started in the business of aviation, but undoubtedly France was leading Europe at this time. The Brazilian-born Alberto Santos-Dumont had flown his Demoiselle aeroplane in Paris in 1906, and the Wright brothers, having reached an agreement with the French Government, visited France three months before Cody's flight at Laffen's Plain, and flew daily public demonstrations. Many influential Britons witnessed this, and others returned for further demonstrations the following year. The French staged the Grande Semaine D'Aviation at Reims in August 1909. Among those present were Generals Sir John French, David Henderson and Sir James Grierson, who were very impressed by demonstrations flown by military pilots attached to the French Artillery and Engineer regiments. But the generals took no immediate action on returning to their desks. When members of the Aero Club of the United Kingdom started travelling to France to learn to fly at the schools established by aeroplane manufacturers, such as Voisin, the Farman brothers and Louis Blériot, they bought French aeroplanes and shipped them back to Britain.

# 3

# THE HILL OF LARKS

The Aero Club began in 1901 when Vera Butler was planning a motoring trip for her father, Frank Hedges Butler, and his good friend the Hon. Charles Rolls. But, before they we due to set out, Vera's Renault caught fire and their outing was cancelled, and a trip in their friend Stanley Spencer's balloon 'City of York' was arranged in its place. Over Sidcup, whilst sipping a glass of champagne, the trio discussed the need for an aeronautical club, along a similar line to the Royal Automobile Club, and set about the task of founding one immediately after landing. At this time, the Aero Club of the United Kingdom's sole interest was amateur ballooning. (The emphasis on amateur is well illustrated by their rejection of Samuel Cody's first application, on the grounds of the entrepreneurial nature of his enterprise. The club would, however, later accept Cody as a member, and then see fit to award him their first gold medal for aeronautical achievements in 1912.)

By the end of the decade the club had received royal approval and become the governing body for all matters aviation in Britain and welcomed exponents of heavier-than-air aviation into its midst. It was also the first such organisation in Britain to accept women as equal members. Frank Butler had been lobbying the War Office to allow the club members permission to use military land for aeronautical experiments, and in February 1909 the club journal, *Flight* (which later evolved into *Flight International*, the aviation industry-standard periodical) was pleased to report, 'The War Office is prepared to grant the club facilities for the use of War Department land for flight trials, providing that there is no interference with military training'.[1]

Among the first Aero Club members to take up the offer was Horatio Claude Barber. This thirty-four-year-old entrepreneur had recently returned home from Canada having made a fortune in silver mines, which he then expanded by 'breaking the bank' at a casino in New York on the journey back to Britain. Although he had no engineering background, or any aeronautical knowledge himself, Barber had some creative ideas and joined forces with the aeroplane designers William O. Manning and Howard T. Wright.

Horatio Barber. (*Flight*)

W.O. Manning. (*Flight*)

# AEROPLANES

Inventors' ideas carried out and
details designed.

Mechanical stability guaranteed.

**HOWARD T. WRIGHT,** 110, High St.,
Marylebone.

Advertisement for Howard Wright
aeroplanes, 1909. (*Flight*)

Howard T. Wright. (*Flight*)

Manning and Wright were both trained electrical engineers who had met in 1908, and discovered a mutual interest in aviation (Howard Wright had established 'the first aeroplane factory for the supply of machines to customers' in Britain, with his brothers Warwick and Walter[2]) and they took Manning onboard as their Chief Designer. In March 1909 Barber, Wright and Manning formed an aeroplane manufacturing company in Britain, which they called the Aeronautical Syndicate Ltd (ASL). They based themselves under the railway arches at Battersea in London, alongside Eustace and Oswald Short. The Short brothers had set up their balloon factory close to Battersea gasworks where there was a plentiful supply of coal gas. The Shorts, who had recently been joined by their brother Horace, were also about to make their first venture into aeroplane construction, having agreed to build copies of Wilbur and Orville Wright's machine in Britain under license. Both ASL and Short Brothers needed somewhere to test their designs, and whilst Shorts went to the Aero Club's flying ground on the Isle of Sheppey, ASL approached the War Office and was granted permission to rent a piece of land measuring approximately 100 square yards on Durrington Down, Salisbury Plain. Barber moved to the nearby town of Amesbury to supervise the construction of an aeroplane shed. He stayed at Ivydene on Salisbury Road, while he obtained lodgings for his chauffeur, Bertie Woodrow, in a cottage behind the Stonehenge Inn in the village of Durrington, one mile to the east of the site that became known as Lark Hill.

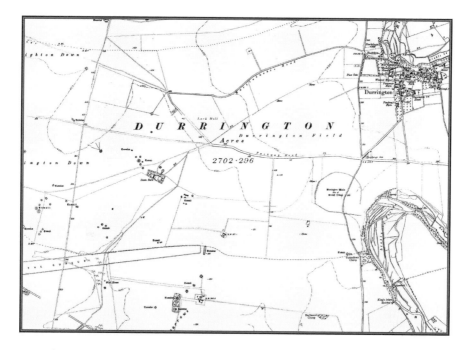

Map of Durrington Down, 1903. (Ordnance Survey)

Lark Hill was a typical area of uneven sloping down land, and even today appears an improbable site for an airfield. But by the simple expedient of providing copious amounts of free beer obtained from the Stonehenge Inn, local military personnel were persuaded to help prepare the site, and with the assistance of one of their steamrollers they created an acceptable flying ground. In June 1909 the tin-shed had been erected, close to the junction with The Packway and Tombs Road, in which ASL could assemble and store their aeroplane, and before long they were ready to start their flying trials.

Their first ASL aeroplane was known simply as Monoplane No.1 and the honour of testing it was entrusted to Bertie Woodrow. Barber said to his chauffeur, 'You drive my car, so you had better drive the aeroplane', to which Woodrow dutifully responded, 'Very good Sir.'[3] But despite Woodrow's best efforts he was unable to get it airborne, for even though the aeroplane was of an advanced design, the 50hp V8 Antoinette speedboat engine, which powered the heavy machine, was not powerful enough to lift it. Disappointed with the failure, ASL sold the monoplane to a businessman from the Midlands, in whose hands it is believed to have flown just once, during which he crashed and wrote it off. Meanwhile, Manning and Wright set about building their second aeroplane.

Aviation pioneers may have been brave men with brilliant ideas, but they were often uninventive when it came to naming their machines, and ASL's mundanely named Monoplane No.2 was ready in the spring of 1910. With shadows of the Cody experience on Laffen's Plain, Woodrow, who had not had any flying training, resorted to taxiing the aeroplane around the airfield at half-throttle to gain experience of how the machine handled on the ground. Allegedly, on 6 March 1910 he hit a tuft of grass and the machine shot up into the air to a height of about 30ft above the ground. Woodrow immediately cut the engine, and pointed the aeroplane at the ground, where the resulting heavy landing damaged the machine's port wing and its undercarriage.

Perhaps whilst recounting this experience, Woodrow persuaded Mr Herbert Bannister, his landlord who was also a cycle mechanic, to join ASL.[4] Monoplane

ASL Monoplane No.2 at Lark Hill, 1910. (*Flight*)

No.2 was repaired and further tests were conducted. These were reported in *Flight* magazine as follows:

> Very quietly, but with much determination to succeed, the Aeronautical Syndicate have, during the past year, been carrying out experiments in Wiltshire with a monoplane of their own design, and finally, after many trials they recently achieved their first flight of several hundred yards. Their machine is peculiar in flying "tail first" . . . Unlike the majority of modern monoplanes (it) has a propeller behind the main planes, which arrangement possesses the advantage of leaving the pilot with an unobstructed view. On making its flight, the machine rose on an even keel at the end of a forty yard run, and covered a distance of a quarter of a mile at 20 to 30 feet above the ground.[5]

When later asked about his first flying experience, Woodrow simply said, 'I just wanted to get the bloody thing back on the ground.'[6] Nevertheless, on 18 March 1910 he accepted his employer's offer of a five-year contract as the company's demonstration pilot, on a salary of £2 a week.

Test flying of Monoplane No. 2 continued until a series of flights, intended to determine the optimum angle of incidence of the foreplane, proved to be the end of that machine. The foreplane had been set at too steep an angle, and after take-off the aeroplane's nose rose higher and higher as the airspeed increased, until the machine flipped over and crashed into a field near to Stonehenge. Thankfully, Woodrow escaped uninjured.

Official Government policy was not to support aviation experiments, however, some members of the Admiralty and the War Office appeared to have had their own agenda when Charles Rolls contacted them. The Hon. Charles Stewart Rolls, the third son of Lord Llangattock, is best known as the automobile salesman who, in 1904, teamed up with the electrical engineer F.H. Royce to create the now-famous motor car marque. An expert balloonist and

Bert Woodrow – arguably the first test pilot in Britain. (Author's Collection)

aviation enthusiast, Rolls had flown with Wilbur Wright at Pau in 1908, and enjoyed a close association with the Balloon School at Farnborough. Having previously purchased balloons from the Short brothers, Rolls was interested to learn they had obtained a license to build copies of the Wright Flyer. He placed an order in February 1909 for their first aeroplane, along with a glider, and immediately declared he was willing to use these two machines to teach Army officers how to fly providing the War Office grants him permission to use land for trials. In so doing, Rolls was breaking a promise he made the Wright brothers that he would not divulge their design secrets to the British Government; nevertheless his offer was enthusiastically accepted by the War Office.

The Army did not start looking for a suitable site for these lessons until October 1909. The first choice, Laffan's Plain, was unimaginative. Rolls rejected it and refused to fly there as he thought the surrounding terrain was unsuitable and, perhaps heeding the lesson provided by Cody, that the trees growing on site were a hazard; and similarly the Aero Club's flying ground on the Isle of Sheppey was crisscrossed with dykes, and dismissed for being too rough. So the Army moved an aeroplane shed from Eastchurch to its training ground on Hounslow Heath (a notorious area to the west of London, once frequented by highwayman, which now lies under Heathrow Airport). Rolls took delivery of his Short-Wright Flyer S.3 on 1 November 1909 at Eastchurch, where it remained until a decision was made on where he should commence training. Five months later, with a mind to purchase a second aeroplane, Rolls secretively sold the S.3 to the War Office for £1,000, and it was towed to Farnborough. A launching rail was laid there, and the first training course gathered at Farnborough on 20 June 1910. The following day, the S.3's engine was started as a demonstration, but no attempt was made to fly on this occasion, and there is little information on any further training being conducted. It is thought Rolls was too focused on his appearance at the forthcoming Bournemouth Air Gymkhana, and so the S.3 was pushed into the back of a shed at Farnborough and is believed to have remained there until it was scrapped some years later.

Meanwhile, Rolls had bought a second aeroplane from Shorts, designated S.8, and had requested it was fitted with an additional rear-stabiliser in addition to the standard foreplane. The new machine was moved to the shed at Hounslow, where Rolls conducted one test flight before being told the War Office were building him a shed on Salisbury Plain, next to that which had been erected by Horatio Barber.

The final deciding factor to use Salisbury Plain for training was quite understandable. Charles Gray, of *The Aero*, described it as 'by far the best stretch of country in England for the training of aviators',[7] and in May 1910 *Flight* announced 'It is practically certain that (Lark Hill) will be the training ground of our military aviators when they get to work.'[8] Unfortunately, Rolls never took up occupancy at Lark Hill. He died on 12 July 1910 at Bournemouth Gymkhana

The Hon. Charles Rolls preparing for the first return crossing of the English Channel, June 1910. (Unknown)

whilst competing for the Alighting Prize – a precision landing contest. An eyewitness describes the circumstances:

> The accident happened just in front of the grandstand, Rolls had ascended higher than was expected, probably to allow himself a longer glide down so that he could steer more easily for the landing spot. He made two circles to gain height, then flew over the motor enclosure at high speed with a strong following wind, round the back of the grandstand into the teeth of the wind, and glided on a steep gradient towards the mark. At a height of 70 feet he stopped the motor and began to glide down at an angle of about 40 degrees, relying on the wind to help him to avoid a long run on the ground; but to check the descent he brought the elevating planes up very sharply. The machine was at a height of 50 feet when the left side of the tail-plane broke away with part of the left of the rudder. There was a sound of splitting wood, and the elevating plane swung back. The head of the machine turned sharply towards the earth then back, and so crashed, upside down from a height of about 30 feet. The crash, witnessed by thousands of silent and horrified spectators, was followed instantly by a loud report in the engine. Rolls was found lying clear of the machine, and apparently unscathed. He was, however, lifeless, and the doctor said that death had been virtually instantaneous from concussion. [9]

Rolls, who had fractured his skull, became the first Briton to be killed in an aeroplane accident. In a surviving notebook, Rolls had written the fateful note, 'sell tail'.[10] We will never know for sure if this referred to the addition to the S.8,

Wreckage of Rolls' Short-Wright at Bournemouth July 1910. (Flight)

but it appears likely he had concluded the addition was not doing the job as well as he would have liked and was preparing to dispose of it. Another Aero Club member, Cecil Grace, agreed to take up the training commitment, but he was to lose his life shortly afterwards when his aeroplane ditched during a race across the English Channel. This race is not to be confused with Blériot's 1909 first channel crossing, an achievement that inspired Capt. John Duncan Bertie Fulton RFA, a young artillery officer. Fulton had served in the army since 1896, and fought in South Africa at Spion Kop, Colenso, Pieter's Hill. He was mentioned twice in dispatches and earned six clasps to his Queen's South Africa Medal. He heard of Blériot's achievement whilst serving with 65th Battery RFA based

at Bulford Camp, near to Lark Hill, and was determined to build his own aeroplane along similar lines to Blériot's machine. He was given special leave by his regiment 'in order to study aviation as applied to military purposes'[11], and was eager to start flying. But finding he was making slow progress with his own machine, he bought a Blériot XI from Claude Grahame-White, using a £250 grant he had recently been awarded by the War Office, which was to be used to improve the firing mechanisms of the field guns. Fulton took over Rolls' shed

Capt. John Fulton RFA. (Unknown)

and, with a little help from another aviator who had also recently arrived at Lark Hill, set about teaching himself to fly.

His mentor was George Bertram Cockburn, a medical research chemist who had been the first student at Henri Farman's flying school. On possibly his first ever trip Cockburn had a lucky escape. One witness said he either pulled the wrong lever, or pulled it the wrong way and the biplane suddenly pitched upwards. The upper wing of the Farman broke and it crashed. This accident may explain later stories that suggest Cockburn taught his students not to fly above 200ft, increasing their chances of survival if they were to crash. Cockburn completed his flying training in 1909, and the thirty-seven-year-old, who had played rugby union for Scotland, bought a Farman III and was the only British competitor to enter the Grande Semaine d'Aviation at Rheims. Whilst at Rheims, Cockburn met the newspaper magnate Lord Northcliffe and the two men discussed how the French authorities were making provisions to teach military officers to fly, and that there was a lack of similar support in Britain. On his return home Northcliffe, who was probably unaware of the discrete arrangements that had been made with Rolls, wrote to his friend the Secretary of State, Lord Haldane on Cockburn's behalf. Events overtook the letter and the Secretary of State's private secretary, Mr A.E. Widdows replied, 'The Army training grounds are very cramped and crowded but a survey was made for the purpose of ascertaining where aeroplane trials could be carried out, and one or two suitable places were found in the Aldershot and Southern Commands. In these localities, responsible aviators are given permission to erect sheds, subject to certain conditions, and to carry out trails, and among others permission has been given to Mr Cockburn.'[12]

Cockburn erected a shed alongside Fulton's and the two men became good friends. When Fulton was ready to take his RAeCC test his Blériot was unserviceable, so Cockburn offered to lend him his Farman. Amazingly Fulton had never flown a biplane until that day. Having lost the services of both Rolls and Grace, the War Office approached Cockburn, the man who had berated them for not considering such training, and asked him to become the army's unofficial flying instructor. Cockburn agreed and offered to undertake the task, free of charge. His first military student was Lieut Philip W. Broke-Smith, who was followed by

George Cockburn. (Unknown)

George Cockburn
sat at the controls of
his Farman biplane.
(*Flight*)

ASL Valkyrie at Lark
Hill. (Unknown)

several others. Then, in April 1911, Cockburn travelled to Eastchurch to teach four naval pilots, selected by the Admiralty, to fly in two Short aeroplanes, similar to that which had been bought by Rolls, that had been kindly donated by Mr Frank McClean. The naval officers were Lieut Charles Samson RN, Lieut Arthur Longmore RN, Lieut Reginald Gregory RN and Lieut Eugene Gerrard RMLI. Later, Gerrard said, of Cockburn, 'He took infinite care with us and none of us so much as broke a wire up to the time of taking our tickets, although afterwards we had some adventures'.[13]

Back in the ASL shed, Barber was preparing to flight-test their third and what was to be their most successful design, known as the Valkyrie. After initial trials in September 1910, ASL moved their flying operations to three new sheds, which they had rented from Blériot on Hendon airfield, where all further development work was carried out (including fitting the first rudimentary dual-control system to an aircraft in July 1911). Over the next two or three years, ASL sold around thirty Valkyries before Barber decided to retire from aeroplane construction in the face of competition from much bigger companies. On ASL's departure from Lark Hill their vacant shed was quickly taken over by one such emerging firm, the British & Colonial Aeroplane Company.

Advertisement for ASL Valkyrie. (*Flight*)

# 4

# The British & Colonial Aeroplane Company

Sir George White was chairman of Bristol Tramways Company and was a very successful and wealthy businessman; he was a philanthropist and a respected figure in his hometown of Bristol. In 1908 he had ordered a Léon Bollée motorcar, for his own personal use, and a number of Charron taxis, for his company to bring into service in the city, from the Parisian motor dealer Emilé Stern. But when only two of the taxis arrived, and no sign of the others, Sir George dispatched George Challenger, one of his foremen, to go and investigate the problem. Challenger arrived in Paris to find the city was abuzz with aviation. Airships were flying overhead; the cinemas were showing aviation films and all the postcards depicted the latest feats of the many French aviators. Challenger's visit coincided with the Wright brothers' first flying demonstration, which was to be staged at Bollée's factory, Le Mans. Stern sent out invitations to his customers and Sir George asked Challenger to go along and send back a report. The report was encouraging, and when Stern invited his customers to a second demonstration at Pau the following year, Sir George attended in person. He returned from France convinced that aviation was now sufficiently advanced to play a significant part in the future of passenger transportation, and intended to become Britain's first commercial producer of aeroplanes.

When this became known his colleagues on the Bristol Stock Exchange thought him mad. However, in a speech to shareholders on 16 February 1910 Sir George announced, 'For some time past, my brother and I have been directing your attention to the subject of aviation, which seems to offer promise of development at no distant date. We have determined to personally take the risk and expense to develop the science from the spectacular and commercial or manufacturing point of view',[1] and so was started the British & Colonial Aeroplane Company (BCAC), later to be better known under the name the Bristol Aeroplane Company.[2]

Sir George White of Bristol. (*Flight*)

The company set up in a converted tram shed on the north side of Bristol, at Filton, with a not insignificant £25,000, raised by investments from the White family. Sir George, his brother Samuel and son Stanley served on the Board of Directors. Sir George's nephews Mr Henry White-Smith was appointed as company secretary, and Sydney Smith as company manager. The facility they created was second to none. When *The Aero* magazine visited the site, their reporter wrote, 'The BCAC works would make most of our constructors green with envy . . . so beautifully are they planned being, with I think only one exception, the only shops actually designed for aircraft work. It has been my fate to see a good many aeroplanes in the making . . . (this is) a sight one could not see anywhere else in England at present.'[3]

Sir George asked Challenger to become the aeroplane company's chief engineer and works manager. Challenger accepted and chose Collyns Pizey, an apprentice in the company's generating station who shared the enthusiasm for this marvellous idea of flight, to be his assistant. Together, Challenger and Pizey handpicked their team from the best coachbuilders, carpenters, fitters and blacksmiths in the Tramways workforce. In March 1910, Sidney Smith took some of the group to Paris to study aeroplane construction techniques and, whilst there, negotiated, through Stern, a license to build in Britain the French Société Zodiac's monoplane and a biplane. Société Zodiac of Paris had been constructing balloons and airships for several years, but when Henri Farman won a FF50,000 prize for the first flight of one kilometer on 13 January 1908 in a Voisin biplane, they decided to expand and build an aeroplane designed by Gabriele Voisin. Coming onto the market towards the end of 1909 with a 'guarantee of flight', the Société Zodiac machine was undoubtedly the most promising option at that time. Sir George hoped to show these machines at the Second Aero & Motorboat Exhibition that was being staged at Olympia in March 1910, but only the biplane arrived in time to go on display in London. They had not even had time to test it, so after the exhibition it was moved to Filton and prepared for flight.

BCAC engaged the services of Belgian Arthur Duray – racing driver and land-speed record holder – as test pilot. The first flight was planned to take place at Brooklands on 30 April, but on the day the aeroplane was still housed

Sydney Smith and the Société Bristol Zodiac. (Bristol Aero Collection)

Advertisement for Bristol Zodiac at Olympia. (*Flight*)

at Filton. The Zodiac was eventually moved to Surrey on 10 May 1910 and installed in Hangar No.17 where it was erected by Sydney Smith and his assistants Leslie Macdonald, Charles Briginshaw and Henri Labouchere. But Duray had been recently injured in a racing accident, so Sydney Smith stepped forwards and, despite not having had the benefit of flying training, took on the task. He attempted to get airborne on numerous occasions but the machines four-cylinder Darracq engine was unreliable and underpowered. New wings were fitted to generate more lift and with these the Zodiac managed a short-hop on 28 May 1910 in the hands of French pilot Maurice Edmond, who had been brought in to replace Duray. Edmond still struggled to get the biplane to do more than skip across the ground. A final attempt to fly was made on 15 June but the undercarriage was damaged, and with that, all testing on the Zodiac was stopped. The five biplanes under construction were scrapped and the order for the monoplane, which had yet to be dispatched from Paris, was cancelled.

As an alternative, Sir George was considering obtaining a license to build a Henri Farman machine, but Challenger persuaded him that he could copy the design, as the French company had recently published detailed, unpatented plans in the aeronautical press. Within days Challenger had drawn up sketch plans and, by utilising Zodiac parts – including its troublesome engine[4] – had completed the first Bristol Standard Biplane within a few weeks. Sir George had written to the Secretary for War, putting all BCACs resources at the sole disposal of the War Office, and had offered an aeroplane for Capt. Scott's Antarctic expedition, but these proposals were declined; the Government stating that it would prefer it if the company traded on the international market. However, in recognition of the need for a site to test the 'new' aeroplane they offered the company a lease on a patch of War Office land on Lark Hill, and flying rights over 2,284 acres of the surrounding landscape to Stonehenge.

Two months before this the War Office had instructed Messrs Harbrow of South London to construct two double sheds on site. To meet this contract Harbrow's adapted a design they had previously used for church halls and set about demolishing three of the temporary structures which the War Office had erected to the south of Cockburn's shed. To accommodate their own trials, BCAC approached Harbrow's and commissioned them to build a further three metal-framed sheds for their own use. It was from these sheds that, early on the morning of 30 July 1910, the Bristol Standard Biplane, which was to be better known as the Bristol Boxkite, was first flown.[5] The honour of piloting it fell upon Edmond, who subsequently reported the machine handled perfectly but, unsurprisingly, commented that the 50hp Darracq engine was, once again, not producing enough power. In response, Sir George asked Stern to find a suitable replacement. He first suggested a Grégoire unit, but eventually BCAC decided to use the 50hp Gnome radial engine, favoured by Farman, and the company signed an agreement with the manufacturer to become their British agent.

Despite Edmond's encouraging comment after the first flight, many inexperienced pilots found the Boxkite a bigger challenge. Charles Turner reported, 'There was no engine throttle, so the Gnome

Advertisement for Harbrow's Flying Sheds. (*Flight*)

British & Colonial Aeroplane Co Ltd Sheds, 1910. (*Flight*)

either ran full out or stopped. The only control was a switch, by switching on and off, the pilot could get a sort of intermittent throttling effect in this way.' The account also describes other design shortfalls:

> There was a front elevator, which was probably not very efficient as a control surface when the machine was flying slowly, but it was useful as a guide to the pilot, in that he could keep it on the horizon and so know whether he was flying level, diving or climbing . . . the pilot had to be fairly smart in getting the nose down if the engine stopped (as it frequently did). The biplane tail was deeply cambered, and therefore carried a great deal of load. Normally, it worked in the slipstream of the pusher airscrew placed but a few feet ahead of it. When the engine stopped the slipstream disappeared, and the tail lost a good deal of lift (which would cause the nose to pitch-up).[6]

When Henri Farman heard of the copies of his machines he threatened to sue BCAC. Sir George filed a defence on the company's behalf, that the larger engine they were using was an improvement and Farman withdrew his action. Challenger and Pizey then set about producing an initial batch of twenty Boxkites. It has been suggested that Farman recognised an association with BCAC was likely to be a better business proposition and attract positive attention for their machines, whereas continuing his high-profile legal action against BCAC might have the opposite effect. This strategy worked, for the two companies subsequently

Advertisement for Gnome aeroplane engines. (*Flight*)

worked together on a number of joint projects. British aviators were excited by the real prospect of a British machine going into mass production, and the War Office realised this was precisely the sort of enterprise they had been waiting for. Responding to yet more lobbying from Lord Northcliffe, they agreed that Sir George's company could demonstrate its Boxkite at the forthcoming Great Autumn Manoeuvres, to be held on Salisbury Plain that coming September.

Boxkites at Lark Hill. (Bristol Airchive)

# LARK HILL MANOEUVRES, 1910

Sir George White recognised that military interest was key to the successful development of his aeroplane company, but British & Colonial needed an intermediary who might give them the same advantage with the War Office that the Short brothers were now apparently enjoying with the Admiralty. In July 1910 he met Capt. Bertram Dickson whilst at the Bournemouth Gymkhana. Dickson was described as a 'Boy's Own' figure of a man; an officer in the Royal Horse Artillery, he had recently been serving as Military Consul in Van, Turkey, surveying and mapping the Persian border. There it is believed he contracted malaria and whilst returning home, on the grounds of ill health, decided to visit his sister who lived in Paris. Whilst there he visited the Grande Semaine d'Aviation de la Champagne, at Rheims in August 1909, where he had the opportunity to see Blériot, Farman and many others fly. He was impressed and immediately enrolled at the Farman School at Mourmelons – the same school where Cockburn had learnt to fly earlier that year. Whilst there he met an officer in the Yeomanry, Lancelot Gibbs, who had flown for Dunne at Blair Atholl, and was now working towards obtaining his Aéro-Club de France certificate. Dickson describes his first solo, in an article published a few years later by *The Boys Own Paper*, which states:

Capt. Bertram Dickson. (David Dickson)

I only took my first actual flight in 1910. It may be that I was slower than some aviators in getting 'on my own', so to speak, though why I can hardly tell. I had been a pupil of Mr Henri Farman, at Mourmelon, since November 1909, and I spent the winter at that celebrated school of aviation. I shall not easily forget 1 February 1910, for on that day I went up into the air for the first time on an aeroplane. Of course the machine was a Farman biplane, and equally of course – no, I don't mind in the least acknowledging it! – I was very nervous at starting. Indeed, for the first few seconds I felt more than one twinge of something – I hardly know what to call it. However, I got much cooler and more at ease after a minute or so; then I went along right enough. I did two laps of the ground, which was, I understand, extremely good for an initial flight. My sensations on reaching terra firma once more were very mixed, but I remember that I felt quite pleased with myself, and proud of my achievement; for one's first actual flight is a memorable thing.[1]

Bertram Dickson passed his flying tests, and he was awarded Aéro-Club de France Certificate No. 71 on 5 May 1910. Four days later he bought a Farman biplane and entered a number of flying competitions across Europe. Within four days he had set a new British flight endurance record (one hour and thirty-three minutes). He entered for a number of flying competitions across Europe and, two weeks later, won the inaugural Schneider Trophy Race at Tours. Bertram's reputation spread, and through the summer he became quite a celebrity on the air show circuit, impressing the crowds with displays at Anjou, Angers and Rouen.

By July 1910 he was being billed as one of the stars appearing at Bournemouth alongside Cody, Rolls, Grahame-White, Moore-Brabazon and his friend Gibbs. Sir George noted that even among this illustrious company Dickson stood out. He was the undoubted master of a crowd-pleasing manoeuvre known as a *vol planés*,[2] which involved turning the aeroplane's engine off and diving towards the ground, pulling up at the last moment to land from a steep glide.

Bertie Dickson in his Farman, 1910. (David Dickson)

GRANDE SEMAINE D'AVIATION

Dickson" en plein vol, sur Biplan H. Farman - Moteur Gnôme

Postcard showing Dickson performing a *vol plané* in the *Grande Semaine d'Aviation*, 1910. (Author's collection)

One journalist noted, 'No one I have ever seen did such *vol planés* in a straight line with such beautiful accuracy'.[3] Dickson himself commented, 'Cutting one's spark in mid-air is like starting down the Cresta Run . . . you know you cannot stop and must go on to the end.' And would later add, 'My feeling after my first *vol planés* resembled those I have felt after killing a lion or rhinoceros that had charged me.'[4] These performances were 'bringing considerable financial reward', as event organisers were willing to pay Dickson up to £500 a time to demonstrate at their displays.[5] As an ex-military man, and a very capable and flamboyant pilot, Dickson appeared to be the very person BCAC was looking for, and he readily accepted Sir George's proposal to join his company and fly the new Boxkite. However, this agreement might have only been short-lived.

Sir George met Bertram again two weeks later at Lanark, where some 20,000 people had gathered to watch the best aviators compete with one another. On Monday 8 August, five days into the event, Dickson was entered in the 'weight-lifting' competition. He had planned to take off with Charles Gray, editor of *The Aero*, as a passenger. Gray weighed 89kgs so to increase the payload, and balance the Farman, Dickson asked that a number of lead sheets be added to ballast. However, for some unknown reason, instead of adding the 19kgs requested, his mechanics placed 44kgs onboard. The biplane was truly over-weight. Dickson managed to get airborne, but immediately had handling problems and a return to earth by crash landing seemed inevitable. Dickson managed to land, albeit heavily, on rough ground and both occupants were thrown clear of the wreckage, shaken, but thankfully uninjured. The same cannot be said of the Farman, which smashed its propeller. Two days later a replacement machine in the shape of a Howard Wright's 'Farman type' was delivered to the airfield. Dickson remained at Lanark for another week and by the time the contest ended on 16 August he had accumulated some £900 in various minor prizes.

Just before travelling to Scotland, Bertram Dickson retired from the Army on half pay, and immediately after the Lanark meeting started his preparations for the Great Autumn Manoeuvres the following month. He deployed to Lark Hill from

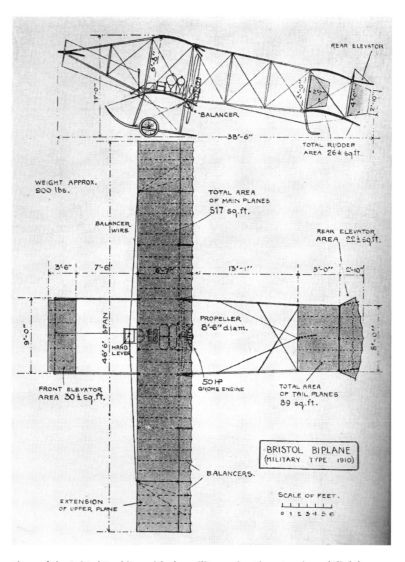

Plans of the Bristol Boxkite, with the military wing tip extensions. (*Flight*)

Filton on 6 September with three newly built Boxkites. Of these, Bristol Boxkite No. 9 had been modified for Dickson to carry a passenger and a larger fuel tank, which necessitated the fitting of detachable extensions to the upper wing that would create more lift; No. 8 had an additional seat fitted and carried a radio transmitter, that had been paid for by Lord Northcliffe; whilst the third machine, a standard Boxkite – possibly No. 7, was there as a spare. Lancelot Gibbs had also agreed to fly and he arrived at Lark Hill on 18 September in his own Maurice Farman Racing aeroplane.

The Great Autumn Manoeuvres were a massive affair, involving up to 75,000 troops, simulating a 'Prussian' invasion force, known as Blue Force, that had landed somewhere in the south-west and was advancing across the country towards London; whilst the Red Force was formed up in a defensive line from Salisbury to Bath to stop their progress. These evolutions were widely reported in the press, and even Pathe News showed film footage of the event[6]. Rather than helping the historical perspective, this extensive media coverage has been causing confusion ever since, as no two contemporary reports tell an identical account of the proceedings. The following is my attempt to relate a sensible, and as accurate as possible, sequence of events.

Monday 19 September was the first day of the manoeuvres, however, strong northeasterly winds and low pressure precluded any flights. The following day started the same, but Dickson flew several times later on that afternoon and these flights were described in *Flight* magazine as follows,

On Tuesday some trial tests were carried out by Captain Dickson, the well-known aviator, with the Bristol biplane he will be using in the forthcoming Army manoeuvres. This aeroplane specially built for the purpose was only commenced on August 17th and yet it was delivered on Saturday last. Early on Tuesday, Captain Dickson took it out for its first trial when it did a fine flight and showed great stability in the air. A few minor adjustments were then made, and the trials were resumed in the evening, when the wind had moderated to about 12 miles per hour. On this occasion Captain Dickson made some magnificent flights for a long distance over the surrounding country at a height of about 200ft, finishing several of them with very fine '*vol planes*' landing on each occasion with great skill and smoothness. In view of the coming manoeuvres these flights were watched with the greatest of interest by a large number of officers from the neighbouring camps, and a considerable number of the public were also interested in this fine exhibition of the new Bristol biplane. In the manoeuvres, Captain Dickson expects to give a number of exhibitions of the use of aeroplanes in warfare, showing their possibilities for dispatch carrying, reconnaissance and observation duties. It will no doubt give the liveliest satisfaction in military circles that the machine to be used in the British Army Manoeuvres will be of British manufacture.[7]

Lord Northcliffe – newspaper
proprietor and lobbyist for aviation.
(*Flight*)

As has already been mentioned, Lord Northcliffe was instrumental in the War
Office agreeing to the BCAC involvement. He had also instructed *The Daily Mail*
to fund the fitting of radio equipment into the second Boxkite (later referred to,
by that paper, as 'The Daily Mail's Scientific Experiment'), and told the editor
to dispatch two newspaper reporters to Amesbury to cover the event. They were
Harry Harper, the newspaper's former theatre and music hall correspondent, who
first become interested in flying after meeting Samuel Cody whilst covering the
'Klondyke Nugget' shows, and who had recently been appointed as the paper's
aviation correspondent; and Mr George Holt-Thomas. Holt-Thomas agreed to
act as the pilots' driver whilst Harper, who had brought along his motorbike,
was briefed to follow Dickson wherever he went and report back on events. On
the Tuesday evening, when Dickson had concluded his test flights at Lark Hill,
Harper rode around the area and located some Blue Force cavalry units before
returning to his hotel in Amesbury, the very same hotel that was being used by
Dickson and Gibbs.

Harper met Dickson in The Crown that evening, but found him 'in a mood of
deep despondency'.[8] Not unreasonably, Dickson had thought he would be briefed
by the Army directing staff on what was expected of them that week, however he
felt he had been 'Cold-shouldered by his former colleagues, the regular officers of
the Army, and regarding himself as merely tolerated at the Manoeuvres as a sop to
Parliamentary questions'.[9] Lacking any instruction or guidance, Dickson and Gibbs

Dickson and Boxkite at the Autumn Manoeuvres, September 1910. (*Flight*)

agreed a plan of action for the following morning. Dickson would take off first
and attempt to locate Blue Force, under the command of General Douglas. After
which he would then proceed to a landing strip that they had been told would be
marked out near the Red Force headquarters at Codford St Mary (7 miles NW
of Salisbury). He would file a report, and Gibbs would follow later. The two pilots
retired early and Dickson booked an early call from the Hall Porter.

The call came at 4.30 a.m., and shortly afterwards both pilots climbed into
Holt-Thomas' car to be driven up to the airfield, hoping to take full advantage of
the early morning calm. However, on passing the Stonehenge Inn they noticed
an autumn frost had settled overnight and that mist was lying in the valleys. On
arrival at the BCAC sheds they found Collyns Pizey and his team of mechanics
had already brought out the Boxkites for them. Dickson wasted no time and
started preparing for his flight, dressing in two woollen cardigans, topped with
a rough tweed jacket, and breeches and overalls on top. He gratefully accepted
Harper's offer of a pair of his motorcycle leggings and the suggestion that he
should further insulate them with sheets of newspaper. Finally, he placed a padded
leather helmet 'of the type work by tobogganists at St Moritz'[10] onto his head and
Dickson was ready to go.

At 5.25 a.m. a mechanic spun the propeller and the Gnome engine burst into
life, in a cloud of smoke and the pungent smell of Castrol, Dickson signalled

to the engineers to release the aeroplane, which rolled forwards down a slight slope before taking off into the autumn mist. Harper describes the scene; 'We lost sight of him quickly in the low-lying mist, but could hear his engine for some time as he steered out across the plain.'[11] Climbing to a height of around 2,000ft and turning southwest towards Stonehenge, Dickson flew on towards the River Wylye, Fovant and Tisbury, before turning north again to Fonthill and onto Codford; a reconnaissance flight of some 30 miles in all. During this trip Dickson spotted the North Somerset Yeomanry, and other Blue Force cavalry units, moving towards Wylye. Corporal Arthur Edwards was with the troops on the ground; 'We were up at the crack of dawn to feed and groom our horses. Before we finished we heard a noise overhead – an aeroplane . . . military discipline collapsed and we stood up waving and cheering. In the excitement the combined noise of our cheers and the noise of the aircraft's engine alarmed the horses, and several broke loose and scattered.'[12]

The Army's Beta airship was present during the manoeuvres, flown by Col Capper, and appears to have been quite effective. The following week *Flight* reported, 'On the previous Monday she sailed over to Salisbury and scouted during the afternoon. A slight mishap with the engines kept her "confined to barracks" on Tuesday, but on Wednesday, Thursday and Friday practically the whole of Somerset, Dorset and Wiltshire were covered during reconnoitring operations, in all about 700 miles.'[13] Beta had a great advantage over the Bristol Boxkites in that she was fitted with wireless telegraphy equipment to pass

Dickson overflying Blue Forces on 21 September 1910. (*Flight*)

messages back to the staff on the ground. Without that advantage, Dickson had to fly back to Red Force headquarters, land, and make his report. Approaching Codford St Mary he looked around for the landing strip, but it had not been laid out as expected. Dickson circled for a while, and then put down on a level hilltop a short distance away nearby known as 'The Bake'. Immediately on landing, an officer and three troopers of the 11th Hussars, attached to Blue Force, approached him. He informed Dickson he had landed in 'enemy territory', however, with great presence of mind, Dickson responded that he was under the command of the directing staff, not the Red Force commander, so was a neutral. When the officer asked him if he had any information, Dickson simply responded, somewhat evasively, he was 'jolly cold and hadn't had breakfast yet'.[14] During this conversation, Holt-Thomas arrived in his motorcar, followed by Harper on his motorbike and, with the Chief Umpire's blessing, the trio departed for Codford village. The Red Force staff officers were having breakfast at The George Inn when Dickson arrived, and he laid out his maps on a small table beside the porch. Harper later wrote,

> As we got out of the car, some of the staff officers came hurrying out from the inn . . . [and] one or two of them were busy lighting their after-breakfast pipes. Out there in the road, standing besides the door of the inn, Dickson described in quick, lucid words just what he had seen while up in the air. The mist had been a drawback for him, but he was able to tell them enough of real significance from a military point of view.[15]

Harper noted some of the officers were standing there with their hands in their pockets, in those days considered a sign of disinterest verging on contempt; but added, their indifference turned to enthusiasm when Dickson began to paint, 'A far more detailed picture of the enemy's movements than they had been able to glean from their cavalry scouts . . . and as a result changed [their] plans.'[16] A reporter with the *Birmingham Gazette*, who also witnessed this briefing, perceptively reported, 'Today should be a notable date in military calendars, for it is the first on which this potent instrument of war has been used in British manoeuvres',[17] and when the officers in Blue Force heard what had happened, one is alleged to have spluttered, 'He's ruined it . . . we might as well all go home!'[18]

Later that morning, as the sun rose higher and the mists cleared, Dickson was asked to get airborne once more. As he had declared himself to the umpires as neutral, he was instructed to ensure he flew over both Red and Blue Force held territory. He took off at 8.00 a.m. and headed south, towards the Blue Forces he had located earlier. He quickly relocated the cavalry units, and thirty minutes later landed in a stubble-field close to the lake at Fonthill Gifford, where he made his way on foot to a nearby house to telephone in his next report. Returning to his aeroplane, he was met by a group of Red Force officers. One of them shouted to his men, 'Keep a sharp look out for enemy patrols', as Dickson discussed with a colonel on the staff the various troop-positions he had observed, using an ordnance map and his sketches. 'Top hole, top hole,' exclaimed the Colonel, 'that's just what we wanted to know.'[19] However, the lookouts were not especially attentive, and Dickson's landing had been seen by a Blue Force patrol who rode up and shot blanks at a number of the Red Force officers. Cpl Edwards[20] was in the patrol, and he later said 'The Boxkite appeared again, circled overhead and landed two fields away. We immediately galloped over, and although too late to prevent Capt. Dickson from phoning information to his headquarters, were able to capture the aircraft and put it out of action.'[21]

Again, the umpires arrived and advised Dickson the information he had passed could not be communicated as the officer had been 'killed'. Dickson approached another, saying 'I must repeat my message, seeing that I inadvertently confided in an officer a moment or two after he had been shot by the enemy.'[22]

Whilst this matter was being resolved a number of senior officers and visiting VIPs led by General Sir John French and the Duke of Connaught arrived, followed shortly afterwards by Winston Churchill, Field Marshall Roberts and Lord Kitchener. Churchill, the Home Secretary, had deliberately broken short a visit to Constantinople and returned to Britain a few days earlier to witness the manoeuvres. He chatted with Dickson for about half an hour, who impressed upon him the part that aviation could play in future naval and military operations. Another visitor to the scene was Capt. Fulton, who had travelled over from his

General Sir John French. (Author's collection)

Winston Churchill MP – Home Secretary. (Author's collection)

Robert Loraine, who also flew during the Autumn Manoeuvres. (Unknown)

shed at Lark Hill to see what was happening.

Dickson flew two more sorties that day, before he returned to Lark Hill and handed over his Boxkite to Lancelot Gibbs. Gibbs had been planning to fly in his Farman, but on arrival at the flying ground that morning had found it unserviceable (no accounts offer any explanation why Gibbs did not fly earlier in either of the two Boxkites that were available at Lark Hill). Gibbs got airborne in the Boxkite, and was able to bring back more useful information on the disposition of the troops Dickson had seen earlier in the day.

A third aviator's involvement should not be forgotten. In the run up to the manoeuvres the intention to use aeroplanes was reported in the *Daily Telegraph*, where it was spotted by Robert Loraine. The well-known actor and enthusiastic aviator, who had served in the yeomanry in the Boer War, would like to have taken part but was committed to open in a play in the West End on the evening of 20 September. However, on completion of the first performance, Loraine swiftly departed the theatre and drove overnight to Amesbury. Arriving early on Wednesday morning, whilst Dickson was conducting his flights, Loraine offered his services to the Blue Force. With Capt. Smart as a passenger he took off later that morning, but an unknown technical problem forced them to land near Shrewton just 7 miles away. Loraine took no further part in the activities that day, and in the afternoon caught a train back to London in time for the start of the evening performance.

At a press conference held at The George in Amesbury that evening, Dickson was more positive than he had been the previous day. Harper filed a report, which the *Daily Mail* published two days later. It read:

I have obtained from Captain Dickson and Mr L.D.L. Gibbs, the two airmen who have demonstrated in England the utility of aeroplanes in warfare, some observations in connection with the reconnoitring flights they have made at the manoeuvres. Captain Dickson said: "It is has been shown that if one army possesses aeroplanes and another does not, the one which has the new arm can place the other at an almost hopeless disadvantage. Therefore all doubt has been set at rest upon one hitherto controversial point – our Army must have the assistance of a properly equipped air corps. My flights were confined to one day. During the course of them, however, I demonstrated that one of the most reliable of present type aircraft can go out upon a definite aerial mission, can pass high over the enemy's head, and can return again with information so valuable that it may change the whole plan of campaign. From my own point of view as the pilot of the aeroplane I established the fact beyond question that no movement of an enemy, however secretly carried out, is likely to escape the observation of the aeroplanist. Aeroplane reconnoitring is not only more informative than the work of the cavalry, but can be done in infinitely quicker time." Mr Gibbs remarked: "Seeing that the tests were carried out without any preliminary experiments, I think they were extraordinarily successful. Upon the first occasion I ascended for reconnoitring work I was able to find a squadron of cavalry that had been located by Captain Dickson and was thus able to confirm his report almost directly after he had made it. It seems to me that it is almost impossible to estimate the value an aeroplane might be in actual warfare'. A critic said to me the other day, "What is the good of equipping ourselves with a lot of machines when a strong wind keeps them all helpless on the ground?" My reply to him was that if the aeroplane scout was to do what he had been asked only twice out of six times he would be of vital service.'[23]

Several observers questioned the organisation and effect of these flights, including Holt-Thomas, whose report of events was in his own words severely critical. But he was not an altogether disinterested party, having business allegiances with the Farman Company. Despite those adverse reports, the general tone of most newspapers was positive, and the flights on Wednesday 21 September 1910 were considered a success. The timing of Dickson's flight was crucial. He had a pre-arranged trip to Milan to fly in an air show and was scheduled to depart from Lark Hill the following day, a commitment he had agreed to before joining BCAC. If he had not been able to fly that day it is likely future aviation development in Britain would have been held back.

It is not clear what happened to Gibbs, however, a few days later, Loraine was approached and agreed to conduct some experimental flights in the Boxkite fitted with the Thorne-Baker radio equipment. He caught the first morning train out of London on Monday 26 September and arrived at Salisbury Station at 8.00 a.m., where he was met by a driver and taken up to the airfield to begin the trial. This would involve tapping out messages in Morse code whilst flying. Loraine had some knowledge of Morse from the time he had spent in the Yeomanry, and had been brushing up on his skills in his dressing room over the weekend. A receiver had been set up in a small room attached to the back of the BCAC sheds, with which it was hoped to pick up any messages Loraine was transmitting. *Flight* continues to describe events, 'Some interesting experiments were made on

Monday by Robert Loraine, who, piloting a "Bristol" aeroplane, was able to send some messages by wireless telegraphy to a temporary station rigged at Lark Hill. The transmitting apparatus was fixed in the passenger seat of the aeroplane, and Mr Loraine operated the Morse key with his left hand whilst he was controlling the machine with his right. Communication was maintained over a distance of about a quarter of a mile, and by way of a start may be considered a valuable achievement.'[24]

The experiment continued for several days, with Loraine travelling backwards and forwards to London for his performances, and then, on 30 September, the ground station picked up a transmission from the aircraft, which was over a mile away. Mr Barron, an employee of Marconi, who was witnessing the trial, excited everyone when he said there was no reason why a well-tuned receiver should not receive messages from 10 to 20 or even 50 miles distance. In a later article, *Flight* added, 'Considerable gratification has been felt at Bristol with the splendid

## THE ACTOR-AVIATOR.

### WHAT HE DID WHILE BRISTOL WAITED.

### "WIRELESS" SUCCESS.

Whilst Bristol people were congregated on the Downs yesterday waiting for Mr. Robert Loraine, that gentleman was engaged on Salisbury Plain in transmitting wireless messages from his airship to the ground.

The new Thorne Baker apparatus was used, and greatly increased efficiency was obtained, the signals being heard when the aeroplane (in charge of Mr. Robert Loraine) was nearly a mile from the receiving station.

A member of the Marconi staff was present and expressed the opinion that, with a tuned Marconi receiver, communication should be easy with the present transmitter up to ten or twenty, or perhaps fifty, miles. The Marconi Company is greatly interested, and has offered to co-operate with Mr. Thorne Baker in further experiments. Their engineer will be present to co-operate in the trials next week, when long-distance communication from the air is anticipated.

Mr. Loraine made several good flights in a Bristol aeroplane lent by the British and Colonial Aeroplane Company, Limited. He is very busy learning the Morse code, and is already quite proficient.

Newspaper clipping reporting Loraine's radio experiment. (Unknown) results obtained in the Army Manoeuvres with the two biplanes of the Farman type, built by the Bristol & Colonial Aeroplane Co. Ltd at Bristol, and piloted by Capt Dickson and Mr Robert Loraine respectively.'[25]

In Milan, Dickson was badly injured in the first ever-recorded mid-air collision on 3 October. Again, this is another incident where reports are confusing. Some say Dickson was competing for a long-distance prize (the organisers were certainly offering a prize to the first pilot to cross the Alps), others that he had completed his demonstration and had got airborne of his own volition 'for a flutter'. What is clear is it was around 4.30 p.m. on the final afternoon of the show, during which Dickson had been performing *vol planés* for excited audiences all week. Dickson collided with an Antoinette that was being flown by the racing driver René Thomas, at a height of about 150ft. The undercarriage of the Antoinette became entangled with the upper wing of Dickson's machine and the two aircraft, locked together, fell to the ground. On impact, Thomas was thrown clear of the wreckage and suffered minor injury, whilst Dickson was crushed under the weight of both aeroplanes. It took some time to remove him from the wreckage, whereupon he was found to have a broken leg and pelvis, which temporarily paralysed him from the waist down; he also had other internal injuries. He was taken to hospital, where it was feared at first he might not recover. However, he was discharged several weeks later, but not before he had missed the opportunity to represent BCAC in the De Forest Cross Channel competition (during which Cecil Grace lost his life). Whether Dickson had been trying to avoid the other aircraft, or if he had not heard Thomas over the noise of his own engine is uncertain; it was thought that the latter's aeroplane was damaged and that Thomas may have been having control problems. Writing at the time, Dickson's friend Charles Gray was of the opinion that, had Bertram been better treated by the Army whilst he was on Salisbury Plain, he might have abandoned the trip to Milan, and remained for the duration of the manoeuvres, and so have avoided this collision. There was already talk in some quarters that the War Office might be persuaded to form an aviation corps and that Dickson was the most likely candidate to take command. However, fate intervened.

Dickson sued Thomas for £4,000 for his injuries, and so Thomas filed his own claim. At the enquiry Dickson was unable to give evidence himself as he had no recollection of events leading up to the accident and the court had little choice but to accept Thomas' account; unsurprisingly, they found in favour of the Frenchman. Dickson was ordered to pay Thomas £600 in damages, and a similar amount to the Antoinette Company. Dickson flew for the first time after his accident at Lark Hill in February 1911, but rarely, if ever, flew again. He was, however, a regular visitor to Salisbury Plain in the course of his work with BCAC and, as we shall see, reported to several government committees on the future potential of military aviation. Dickson died on 29 September 1913 in Scotland. He was staying with friends at Lochrosque Castle near Achanalt in Rosshire

The British & Colonial Aeroplane Company, Limited.

Office and Works:
**Bristol.**

Telegrams:
"Aviation, Bristol."
Codes:
A.I., A.B.C. and Moreing.

Flying Schools:
**Salisbury Plain
and
Brooklands.**

## "BRISTOL"

BIPLANES.          MONOPLANES.

AEROPLANES built to Clients' own designs.

PROPELLERS specially built for any type of
Engine.   WE have made a special study of this
branch of aeroplane work, and produce the most efficient
PROPELLERS at a reasonable price.

The ...

## "BRISTOL"

is the **BIPLANE**

which was specially chosen by

## CAPTAIN DICKSON

for his successful demonstrations at the recent

**ARMY MANŒUVRES AT SALISBURY PLAIN.**

British & Colonial advertisement emphasising the company's successes and links with the city of Bristol. (*Flight*)

when he died suddenly (his family suspect he succumbed to a stroke probably as a result of injury sustained in the accident). His death is today recorded in the estate's Game Book.

Naturally, BCAC made the most of their success at Lark Hill. By November 1910 the company had employed Henri Jullerot and Maurice Tétard as company test pilots, and they were staging spectacular flying displays at Durdham Down in the heart of Bristol. Their factory at Filton was soon producing Boxkites at a rate of two a week, which were sold for £1,100 each. The company intended to set up flying schools at Lark Hill and Brooklands, and asked for permission to build a further two double-bay sheds at Lark Hill, which had, by then, been confirmed as the Army's principle aviation base. Approval was given, providing the wide gap between the buildings was maintained to comply with the wishes of Sir Edmund Antrobus, on whose land the Stonehenge monument stood, so that the new structures would not obscure the view from the monument of the summer solstice sunrise.[26] Everyone at Lark Hill had come to know this space as the Sun Gap.

# 6

# THE POSITION OF THE SUN GAP

The existence of the Sun Gap is unquestionable, however, over the years some uncertainty as to its exact location has arisen. The monument standing on site today claims to mark the position, based on the perceived wisdom that it lay to the south, between the Government sheds and the original BCAC sheds, and there is clear photographic evidence that such a space existed. Local Amesbury historian Norman Parker was adamant that this is the correct position as related to him in distant conversations with some who flew from Lark Hill at the time. However, no supporting documentary evidence has come to light that this was indeed the Sun Gap, and a sketch map enclosed with letters written by Group Captain Peter Dye RAF (later Air Vice Marshall Dye, Director General of the RAF Museum, and President of the aviation historical society Cross & Cockade International) in 1997 suggested the Sun Gap was located further north, closer to The Packway.

Peter Dye's assertion was apparently based on the geographical alignment that can be checked today, by drawing an extended line through the Altar Stone in the centre of the Stonehenge ring and the outlying Heel Stone over to the flying ground. This suggests the Sun Gap was actually at the northern end of the Government sheds, and in some photographs there is an indication of another space in that position.

In fact, in an article written for Cross & Cockade by Peter Wright, he states,

When the application to erect the Bristol sheds was made, it was intended they would be sited next in line south of the single ex-Rolls military shed. However this was not approved by the local authority as the new sheds would have obscured the natural horizon as viewed from the Stonehenge Altar stone at the Summer Solstice.[1]

If the Sun Gap is located to the north, as it now seems it probably was, there is no explanation why the second confusing gap was left to the south. Visitors to the site today will notice a marked gradient north to south as they proceed along Wood Road, steepening as they approach the BCAC sheds. Perhaps, in

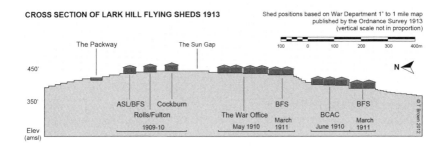

Elevation showing the relative position of the Lark Hill flying sheds in 1911. (Author)

complying with War Office requirements, it proved impractical to build the sheds on the sloping and uneven ground immediately south of the Government sheds.

In 1911, BCAC had already adopted the ASL shed for the Bristol Flying School, so when it was ready to expand its operation it would have been logical for them to erect their new sheds in the northerly gap. That option would have been unacceptable if that space is the Sun Gap. It might have been possible to erect one of the new, smaller pair of sheds in the southerly gap, but necessary to erect the other pair at the opposite end, straddling their existing structure. All this remains, of course, conjecture. The simple facts are that the Sun Gap existed, although truthfully it served no direct purpose to aviation. Its precise location between the fourteen sheds that were in position on site by the summer of 1911 is rather academic and not really worthy of further prolonged discussion.

# 7

# THE FIRST MILITARY AEROPLANES ARRIVE

Early in 1910, Colonel Joseph Laycock and the Duke of Westminster donated a Blériot XII monoplane to the British Government, but their gesture was hardly as philanthropic as it might seem. The previous August, Claude Grahame-White had seen Louis Blériot competing in two of these machines at The *Grande Semaine d'Aviation de Champagne* at Bethany, near to Rheims (subsequently known as the Rheims Aviation Week). After a notable performance in the speed competition, the slower 40hp Anzani powered XII finished in second place to Glen Curtis. However, Blériot was not satisfied with 'runner-up', and took off later that day in the 60hp E.N.V powered machine and set a new world speed record and Grahame-White told Blériot he wished to purchase the aeroplane after the event. On the last day of the competition Blériot had the prestigious final race, but horrified spectators watched on as a fractured fuel-pipe spilt petrol onto a hot exhaust soon after take-off and the aeroplane burst into flames in mid-air. Thankfully, Blériot landed safely and walked away from the burnt-out wreckage, with only minor burns – he agreed to build Grahame-White another. Whilst waiting for this machine to be completed, Grahame-White, a qualified motor mechanic, worked in the Blériot factory to gain knowledge of aeroplane design and construction.

When his Blériot XII was delivered in November he nicknamed the machine 'White Eagle', and although he had not yet received any instruction could not resist taking a few 'hops' before he started flying training under M. Alfred Leblanc at Pau. On 28 November 1909, whilst being flown by Blériot himself, the XII was damaged during a forced landing, and the constructor immediately declared the aeroplane 'dangerously unstable' and told Grahame-White he would replace it with two of his XI type machines. Despite this condemnation, a few months later Blériot appears to have been quite happy to offer the same XII, or a similar, to Laycock and Westminster. However, it is possible that Laycock,

Grahame-White's Blériot XII 'White Eagle' at Etampes, c.1909. (Unknown)

Lieut Reginald 'Rex' Cammell RE. (Unknown)

who was the English agent for E.N.V Motor Syndicate, the manufacturer of the engine fitted to this machine, might have influenced his decision.

In June 1910 Capper looked among his staff at the Balloon School for a suitable individual who could be sent to the Blériot factory at Étampes to accept the machine. He chose an enthusiastic young Royal Engineer Lieutenant called Reginald 'Rex' Cammell, who had some experience on kite-gliders and had piloted the Army's Beta airship. Cammell had unsuccessfully requested to join Dunne's team at Blair Atholl in 1908, and flown as a passenger with Cody, but otherwise had no experience of powered fixed-wing flight. This did not really matter as he was being sent to simply inspect and accept the aeroplane, whilst another officer, Lieut James Boothby, Royal Scots, had already been chosen to conduct test-flying in Britain.[1]

However, Cammell had other ideas. His stated personal goal was to perform, 'Some preliminary assays with the machine, until satisfied that I should be able to fly it on return to England'.[2] Cammell arrived at Etampes on the morning of 29 June 1910 but found the airfield empty. He waited until lunchtime when a small team of mechanics arrived with the aeroplane on a cart, and set about assembling it. By 5.00 p.m. the aeroplane was ready, but still there was no sign of Blériot, who did not arrive until 6.30 p.m., and after exchanging pleasantries the whole party retired for the evening.

It was another two days before Cammell had his first opportunity to see the Blériot XII fly. Blériot was determined to get airborne despite the facts that its E.N.V engine had not been running smoothly, and offered to fly Cammell as a passenger. Again and again the XII skipped across the rough ground, but the engine could not develop enough power for the aeroplane to take-off. All attempts at flight ended when the aeroplane bounced so heavily it caused the undercarriage to collapse. The mechanics who gathered around said it would take eight days to repair; this was to be the beginning of a frustrating five weeks wait.

Despite Cammell sending regular reports back to Farnborough, concerns were growing that Laycock had not yet paid Blériot. Cammell wrote to Capper, 'It appears that by the terms of the contract, I am bound to pay for it as soon as it is handed over me. Blériot refuses to break through the terms by sending in a bill to you, and will not hand the machine over until it has been paid for.'[3] In order to kill time, Cammell arranged to visit the Salon de l'Aviation at Rheims. Here he met Capt. Williams, a fellow officer who he described 'as something to do with E.N.V',[4] and from him learned that the XII had originally been built with a 40hp engine, however, keen to increase its maximum speed, Blériot ordered it replaced with a 60hp unit and had the wings cut down in size to reduce drag. The modification was successful, but at a price. Blériot set several speed records, but the machine's handling had been seriously compromised. Williams informed Cammell that Blériot once told Grahame-White that, as a beginner, 'it was about a 1,000 chances to one he would smash it to smithereens at his first attempt.'[5]

Cammell returned to the factory at Étampes where he found, frustratingly, that no progress whatsoever had been made on repairing the XII. In fact, work on manufacturing the required parts had not even begun. What is more, Blériot had departed for England to take part in the Bournemouth Gymkhana. In his frustration he wrote to Capper, 'What is to be done with these liars? I am really losing every shred of patience and temper I ever possessed.'[6] Cammell went on to explain that he had arranged, on his own initiative, a course of flying lessons in a Blériot XI. He added he was willing to pay for the lessons, at a rate of 40F per hour plus breakages, from his own pocket. He also expressed for the first time his desire to fly the machine once it had been delivered (and of course the flying training he had arranged would help his case).

Cammell's first flying lesson was with M. Ferdinand Collin on 20 July. His progress was good, and in his next letter to Capper wrote, 'I shall be quite able to manage the machine now; that at least is one good result of the delay.'[7] Eventually, the XII was ready. It flew on 24 July but was forced to land in a cornfield and in the process damaged its tail plane. Blériot and Cammell flew together on 29 July, but once again the flight ended in a heavy landing and more damage. Understandably, Cammell's final report to Farnborough was unfavourable. He stated the XII was inherently unstable, and that he thought its engine was badly out of tune, and that its angle of descent in a glide was dangerously steep. Cammell's work done, he returned to Farnborough, leaving the XII in France to be packed into a crate and shipped over to Wiltshire.

At 3.00 p.m. on 6 October a small group of Royal Engineers stepped off the train from Farnborough onto the platform at Amesbury station. Some of the party travelled up to Lark Hill, where they took over one of the government sheds and set about erecting tents for their own accommodation. The remainder loaded the Blériot XII, which had arrived earlier that same day, onto a horse-drawn cart. Whilst en route to Lark Hill, a strong gust of wind caught the crate and tipped the whole cart over. Fortunately, the aeroplane was undamaged and the sappers were able to right the cart and it continued on its way. The following day they set about assembling the aeroplane in preparation for flights; but they were unable to run the engine, as they had not brought any castor oil or fuel with them. It was eventually fuelled and ready to run on 8 October 1910.

The engineers who travelled to Lark Hill were under the command of Lieut Cammell, and whilst Boothby had travelled with them, it was Cammell who had responsibility for deciding who would fly the machine, and in this he was to be guided by the instruction he had received from Capper to, 'let Boothby have a go from time to time.'[8] So, it was on 9 October that the Blériot was towed from Lark Hill to the foot of Knighton Down (2.5 miles NW of the airfield) and Cammell flew a number of flights from there. The first trip was a short three-minute hop and, having ventured slightly further away on the second flight, he got lost until he recognised the unmistakable form of Stonehenge and was able to re-orientate himself from that and return to the airfield. Several other flights followed, the longest was of just fifteen minutes duration, interspersed with engine ground runs, which Cammell entrusted to Lieut Boothby. The final flight of the day ended in a heavy landing after just eight minutes when, owing to poor forward visibility, Cammell was forced to make a steep turn to avoid telegraph wires and a collision with the tin cookhouse. Cammell's knowledge of the Blériot XII was increasing, as was that of his ground crew who had nicknamed the machine the 'Man-Killer'.

Cammell continued the test flights, but admitted he was having difficulty maintaining altitude when flying over undulating terrain, which he said, made it difficult to assess whether he was climbing or descending, 'I have often felt that I must be falling rapidly, when really I was only coming to a hill'[9] (the instrumentation fitted to early aircraft was rudimentary and few, if any, had a reliable form of altimeter). After making a heavy landing on 28 October Cammell showed some initial reluctance to accept responsibility, however he eventually admitted it was his fault and wrote, 'I greatly regret the accident which is primarily due to, of course, to my own inexperience . . . my first idea was to blame the machine, but on further reflection it was almost entirely due to me trying to climb and turn at the same time without accelerating the engine.' But Jullerot reminded him in a consolatory manner, the popular flying adage of that time was, 'A pilot's no good, until he's cracked wood.'[10]

Blériot XII, 'The Man-Killer' at Lark Hill, 1910. (*Flight*)

The Blériot XII was in the shed for three weeks being repaired, but no sooner had it emerged than it was damaged again on 22 November. There was no way Cammell could be blamed for this as a hot water pipe came off one of the cylinders in flight, covering the pilot in scalding hot water. One week later he was asked to fly the machine to Farnborough – a flight that would be his first cross-country trip. Taking off in thick mist, he immediately noticed a drop in fuel pressure and had to start pumping fuel to the engine by hand. Cammell remained in the vicinity of the airfield hoping the weather might improve; however, he landed again after about forty minutes, cold and tired. By lunchtime the mist had cleared sufficiently for a second attempt. Intending to follow the Salisbury to Basingstoke road, Cammell took a small detour to avoid some horses, but when setting course again picked up the Winchester road by mistake and got lost. Correcting his error, he was following the railway line towards Micheldever when turbulence forced him to land near North Waltham. At 3.00 p.m., whilst preparing to take-off and complete his journey, he discovered a suspension wire on the wing was broken.

Whilst trying to fix this wire, a mechanic, who had caught up with him, broke the eye off the turnbolt and they decided to cover the aeroplane with a tarpaulin, and proceeded by train to Farnborough to collect replacement parts. However, on their return to the aeroplane the fuel pressure was still worryingly low and the engine shed a bolt on start-up, so they returned to Farnborough again and prudently made arrangements for the machine to be collected the following day and complete its journey by road. In a report published in *The Aero* the following January, the writer stated, 'That so capable and versatile an aviator . . . [as Cammell – the magazine mistakenly used Fulton's name] . . . should risk his valuable life on a machine which is so dangerous, owing to its low centre of gravity, that the type has been condemned and given up its designer.'[11] At Farnborough, the Superintendent of His Majesty's Balloon Factory, Mr Mervyn O'Gorman, had recently engaged the services of a promising designer by the name Geoffrey de Havilland. Seizing the opportunity, de Havilland was given permission to 'reconstruct' the Blériot XII (which was interpreted as approval for a complete re-design) and the aeroplane re-emerged in June 1911 designated SE.1. [12] The SE.1 incorporated so many new designs and ideas with the original unreliable engine, serial number 13, still fitted, that it too, predictably, came to grief on 18 August 1911.[13] Since its re-emergence it had only been flown by de Havilland, however, the Assistant Superintendent at the Balloon Factory was keen to get involved – a wish which proved to be fatal. *Flight* magazine reported on 26 August 1911:

> The sympathies of all interested in British aviation will be with the little band of experimenters at the Army Balloon Factory at Farnborough in the loss sustained by the fatal accident on the 18th to Lieut Theodore Ridge. His experience in the air had mostly been with dirigibles constructed at the factory of which he was the assistant superintendent, but a short time ago he qualified for his brevet on a biplane. The evidence given at the inquest on Monday last, when a verdict of 'Death by misadventure' was returned, rather showed that the accident was another case of the danger of the over-confidence of inexperience. After seeing several flights successfully made by a mechanic, he decided to try the machine himself, although he was warned by the designer, as well as the engineer at the factory, not to do so. He, however, insisted on going, as he felt confident he could manage it. He went for a short flight, and on returning stopped the engine to come down, and then started to make a sharp turn, which he had been especially warned not to do. The machine by this manoeuvre lost its balance and fell to the ground, the pilot being pinned under the debris, and so severely injured that he died the same night in the Connaught Hospital.[14]

The 'Man-killer' had eventually lived up to its nickname. It reappeared from the factory one more time, but is thought never to have flown in this last reincarnation.

After his tribulations with 'White Eagle', Cammell spent December 1910 practising at Lark Hill for his RAeC test. Having only previously flown monoplanes, Cammell took to the biplane Boxkite with ease, and was 'able immediately to show complete control of the machine'.[15] He was awarded his certificate on 31 December, and immediately begun trials with the Dunne-Capper monoplane. Based on a development of the glider used in the trials at Blair Atholl in 1908, this machine had a single overhead, complex arrow-shaped wing. It was kept at Lark Hill into the spring of 1911. Both Cammell and Capper

Dunne-Capper monoplane testing at Lark Hill, 1911. (J. Fuller)

were hoping to carry out trials on this machine; however, these were delayed when Cammell was caught out by a gust of wind, and the aeroplane tipped onto its nose. It was repaired, a third skid fitted to improve its ground stability, and within a few days it was ready for further tests. Accounts of these vary, and it is uncertain whether the machine took off for any meaningful flights at all; however, what is certain is it was not Dunne's most successful design.

Another experimental aeroplane at Lark Hill was the Carter biplane, which arrived early in January 1911. A less radical machine than the Dunne, it was powered by an eight cylinder 60hp engine built by the Nonpareil Motor Co. of Birmingham. The aeroplane's owner and designer flew a few short hops, before deciding it needed more power. He departed for the midlands, 'for certain alterations to be carried out'[16], vowing to return but never did, and nothing more was heard of either Mr Carter or of his machine.

That spring, Cammell bought a more reliable Blériot XXI, which was powered by a 70hp Gnome engine, which he kept and used at Lark Hill. In design it was similar in arrangement to the workmanlike Blériot XI, but with side-by-side, two-seater aeroplane that had a certain elegance; although, when George Cockburn first saw it he described it as weird and wonderful. Having picked up his new machine from Hendon on 21 May, Cammell set off for Lark Hill, via Farnborough, where he planned to stop overnight. His flight towards Salisbury Plain was interrupted by an overheating engine, which necessitated a landing near Basing; eventually arriving at Lark Hill in failing light sometime after nine o'clock that evening. Apparently, such was the reliability of all pre-war aircraft.

# BRISTOL FLYING SCHOOL

After the Great Autumn Manoeuvres, BCAC decided it would establish flying schools, and wrote to the Government offering to train 250 army officers a year at a discounted rate for the War Office, and a similar number of naval officers for the Admiralty. Both services turned down the offer; the War Office was happy to continue to recruit pilots who had funded their own initial training, whilst the Admiralty was making its own arrangements for instruction at Eastchurch. Ironically, this rejection provided BCAC's new flying schools with a different opportunity, and when ASL departed from Lark Hill, the company moved into Barber's shed from where it hoped to attract many young army officers from the nearby camps at Bulford and Tidworth. The first student to earn a Royal Aero Club Certificate at Lark Hill was none other than Capt. John Fulton, on 15 November 1910, and Lieut Cammell, who had been receiving tuition in George Cockburn's Farman, followed before the end of the year.

The Bristol & Colonial Aeroplane Company was hoping to enter one of their aeroplanes into the Michelin Cup in 1911. The pilot of the aeroplane was to be Mr Graham-Gilmour, a rather outrageous character who arrived at Lark Hill early in the New Year. The first task for the mechanics in the Bristol sheds was to replace the Gnome engine for a more powerful E.N.V unit that Graham-Gilmour had been lent by Mr O.C. Morrison, an evolution they completed in just a few days. The aeroplane was test-flown by Graham-Gilmour and M. Tetard.

In the February, Sir George White arranged a press day at Lark Hill to launch the Bristol Flying School, during which the school's new chief instructor M. Henri Jullerot took up many of the journalists. Among the journalists visiting Lark Hill was one Charles C. Turner, who had been writing about aeronautics for *The Observer* since 1908 and was also a keen balloonist. Turner wrote of how Sir George White had created 'the biggest school of flying'[1] by gathering a staff of aviation experts, and had recruited the best French flying instructors. During the Press Day, Archibald Low flew Turner over Stonehenge, and his first experience of aeroplane flight persuaded him to take flying lessons himself.

Cover of *Flight* magazine following Sir George White's press day at Lark Hill, February 1911. (*Flight*)

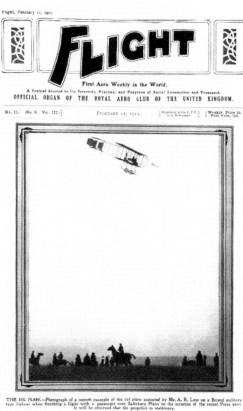

Turner arrived back in Wiltshire on 19 February and booked into The George Hotel in Amesbury, which he noted was 'almost monopolised by the flying men, the staff of the school and pupils'.[2] Activity at Lark Hill was intense. Early starts were the norm as the aeroplanes were easier to handle in still or light air. Every morning, pupils and staff would be driven up to the airfield in the back of an open car. In his later memoirs, *The Old Flying Days*, Turner recalls that when conditions were unsuitable for flying, as they often were, the students would retire to the aircraft sheds, where Collyns Pizey would explain the workings of the Gnome engine or they would help out with any repairs. Otherwise they would conduct imaginary flights whilst sitting on the ground, getting used to the aircraft controls; and when they had had enough of aviation, pupils played football, walked on the downs, or sometimes went skating in Salisbury – an activity which Jullerot felt was 'more dangerous than flying'.[3]

The airfield attracted on-lookers, and the villagers who turned up to watch the aircraft treated the 'flying brotherhood' as heroes. Turner says boys and girls 'besieged The George, bringing their autograph books for us to sign'.[4] Such was their popularity, the Bishop of Salisbury felt inclined to issue a warning to young people in the diocese not to associate with any of the pilots. Bad weather, principally strong winds, kept Turner on the ground for two weeks before his first flight. This was completed in a Boxkite, in which he sat behind the instructor and, by leaning over his shoulders, could place his hands on the controls, as there were no dual-control fitted aircraft at this time. This technique meant the pupils' first solo flight was also the first time they had to work the rudder pedals in flight. This was perhaps not as large an obstacle as might be thought, for pupils were instructed not to attempt any turns, and on such flights the rudder was used solely

Amesbury bus –
bringing students to
the flying ground.
(*Flight*)

to keep the aeroplane flying in a straight line. Turner describes that momentous trip as follows, 'The mechanic starts up the propeller and you raise your right hand as a signal to the mechanics who are hanging onto the machine to let go. And then there's nothing for it: you've got to attempt that flight . . . the machine began to move forwards . . . I could see the ground sweeping past . . . and kicked off. I was off the ground.'[5] Stanley White once suggested to his grandson before a first solo flight that the pilot was instructed to, 'shut his eyes on take-off until all the bumping stops, for then he would surely be airborne'.[6]

A contemporary Eric Furlong, who was taught to fly at Hendon, highlights another weakness in early instruction. Furlong described taxiing backwards and forwards across the airfield, blipping the throttle and endeavouring to keep the machine in a straight line, and in the process rising, at times, into the air 2 or 3 feet. His instructor frowned upon these hops, but Furlong soon realised it was all part of the training process. He goes on to describe flights when he was allowed to get airborne properly:

> At an altitude of approximately 50ft left- and right-hand turns were practiced above the airfield. In those days the instructors knew nothing of aerodynamics and in blissful ignorance, taught manoeuvres that were later considered suicidal. Instead of banking to effect a turn, pupils were instructed to fly absolutely straight and then kick either left or right rudder in when they wanted to change direction. This upset the aerodynamics of the aircraft, the nose dipped and the machine skidded round in the air until it faced the direction from which it had come. The pupil then came into land, taking off again immediately and repeated the process . . .[7]

These unbalanced turns were likely to result in the aeroplane entering a stall, from which it would be impossible to recover at such a low height (even if stall recovery was understood and taught, which it was not).

The instruction may have been rudimentary, but then so were the aeroplanes. Several accounts describe the lack of instrumentation. Christopher Draper writes,

Students and instructors at Bristol Flying School at Lark Hill. (*Flight*)

There were three main instruments. A small glass, in which it was possible to see the oil pulsating showing that the oil pump was doing its job. Fitted to one of the outside struts there was a simple air-speed indicator, consisting basically of a small, engraved metal plate and a pointer. The pressure of the airflow moved this pointer up and down the short scale on this plate, giving a very rough idea of the speed of the plane. The third 'instrument' was a piece of string about eighteen inches long, tied to the trailing edge of the elevator. In a Boxkite the elevator was on outriggers about six feet in front of the pilot's seat, and this piece of string blew back in the pilot's line of sight during flight. If it moved sideways, up, or down, it showed at once that the aircraft was not flying straight.'[8]

Philip Broke-Smith says, 'Until altimeters could be obtained, height had to be judged by an aneroid barometer tied onto the machine [and] compasses were obtained from marine instrument makers…' (the first compasses were fitted to the Air Battalion Boxkites by Mr E.H. Clift in June 1911).[9] Things were no more advanced at the end of a flight, one pilot commenting, 'Aviators have been obliged to provide their own means of braking by jumping out of their seats and robbing the machine of its forward momentum by the vigorous application of their feet as friction brakes.'

Today, visitors to Lark Hill flying ground often comment on the undulating nature of the site, but this had the benefit of an easier downhill take-off, and, in still winds, an uphill landing could be made retarding the aeroplane before it arrived at the sheds. But that was not always the case. Later in his life, Turner wrote an article for *Flight* magazine comparing flying training during the Second World War with his experiences at the Bristol Flying School. He wrote,

In the course of my lessons I only had one mishap. One morning, someone else was flying, when a thick mist suddenly blotted out the scene. We were all listening anxiously to the sound of the engine away in the distance. Suddenly it stopped, and we went out to explore, fearing the worst. However, all was well. The pilot had made a safe landing where the level of the land was somewhat lower. There we all stood, and waited for the mist to clear away, and when it did Jullerot said to me, 'Take it over. Turner.' Nothing loath, for this was indeed a mark of confidence, I got into the machine, then looking round with some doubt, for the ground was tussocky heather instead of smooth turf, and I wondered whether I could take off. But I managed it, and was soon flying confidently in the now sunlit air. Alas! Satisfaction was brief. The mist came down, rose up or else formed all about me. At any rate, I could not see a yard beyond that delicate front elevator, and in a few moments I was completely lost as to locality. For what seemed an age I flew round wondering what I was to do; swiftly, my difficulties increased. I did not like to land, for I had no idea of the direction of the sheds. But fate took charge. Suddenly I found myself heading straight for telegraph wires. Then in a slight clearing of the mist I found myself looking down on a sort of quarry. Turning back more or less in the direction from which I had come, I was confronted by two lots of telegraph wires converging on each other. In fact there seemed to be telegraph wires everywhere. So I decided to land, and managed this with a steep-banked descent and sudden left turn to right the machine before impact. I did not quite succeed, but the only damage was a broken skid. I waited until breathless party, headed by Jullerot, arrived, not disguising their satisfaction that I was not hurt.[10]

Just before Turner started at Lark Hill, the Royal Aero Club extended its requirement to obtain a flying certificate, which meant he had to complete a little more training before he was ready to take his test on 23 April 1911. Taking off that Sunday evening in extremely gusty conditions with wind speeds up to 30kts, he was required to fly five figures-of-eight, but every time he turned downwind the aircraft lost height dramatically and was blown towards the sheds, on one occasion to avoid them he had to fly through the Sun Gap. After landing he received 'a great ovation' and Cdr Harry Delacombe, who was observing on behalf of the RAeC, noted he had never before seen a certificate flight undertaken in such difficult conditions. Perhaps based on this hair-raising experience, Turner departed from Lark Hill vowing he would never fly a fixed-wing aeroplane again and returned to his original interest, ballooning. Actually, he did fly an aeroplane once at Brooklands about a year later, but as if to confirm his dislike that was his last ever flight in a fixed-wing machine. Instead, he completed a number of record balloon flights and became an officer in the Kite and Balloon Section of the Royal Naval Air Service during the First World War.

Lieut Connor – an outstanding student at Lark Hill, who remained there after training with the Air Battalion. (*Flight*)

Many others shared Turner's experience with the winds on Salisbury Plain, and the regular bulletins, 'From the British Flying Grounds' published by *Flight*, relate how the flying was frequently halted by bad weather. In February 1911, Lieut Daniel Connor, a promising student at the Bristol Flying School, was flying solo at about 200ft, when the wind got under the starboard wing of his machine and flipped it onto its side and his machine slid towards the ground. Connor attempted to right the machine but it tipped forwards and threw him out onto the ground. Amazingly he only sustained a few bruises and quickly recovered. He passed his RAeC certificate test a few days later and remained with the military aviators at Lark Hill. Another notable pilot learning how to fly at the Bristol Flying School around this time was Robert Smith-Barry. A pupil

Maurice Tetard flying a Boxkite from Lark Hill, 1911. (unknown)

Aerial photograph of the flying sheds at Lark Hill. (Sir George White)

Bristol Flying School advertisement. (*Flight*)

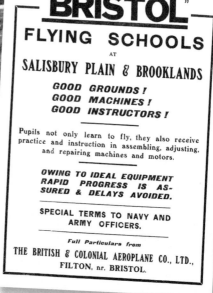

"BRISTOL"
FLYING SCHOOLS
AT
SALISBURY PLAIN & BROOKLANDS

GOOD GROUNDS !
GOOD MACHINES !
GOOD INSTRUCTORS !

Pupils not only learn to fly, they also receive practice and instruction in assembling, adjusting, and repairing machines and motors.

OWING TO IDEAL EQUIPMENT RAPID PROGRESS IS ASSURED & DELAYS AVOIDED.

SPECIAL TERMS TO NAVY AND ARMY OFFICERS.

*Full Particulars from*

THE BRITISH & COLONIAL AEROPLANE CO., LTD., FILTON, nr. BRISTOL.

of Henri Jullerot, Smith-Barry recalls being fined £15 for repairs to a Boxkite he damaged in a heavy landing. Smith-Barry went on to obtain his RAeC certificate in November 1911, and the following year applied to join the RFC. Whilst serving at Gosport, he devised a systemtemic method of flying training that was widely adopted and still the basis for instruction today. He also invented a simple device known as the 'Gosport Tube', that solved the in-flight communication problem between an instructor and his student. This consisted of a hollow rubber pipe running between the instructor and student's helmets, so the student could hear the instructor's comments… but perhaps relevantly could not respond. Lark Hill and Brooklands were the principal flying training schools for military pilots through 1911 and most of 1912 when the Central Flying School opened at Upavon. Even then, for another two years, many would-be naval and military pilots passed through the doors of the Bristol Flying Schools and were paying for their initial training.

## Picture the Scene

Wiltshire has links with photography going back to William Henry Fox-Talbot. Henry, who lived at Laycock Abbey in the nineteenth century, was MP for Chippenham, but is mostly remembered as the inventor of the photographic printing process and creator of the earliest known surviving negative. One of the factors that keep the story of Lark Hill alive, is a collection of excellent contemporary photographs taken by a later exponent of Fox-Talbot's process, Thomas Fuller of Amesbury.

Fuller set up a photographic business in Amesbury in 1911, taking portrait photographs of military personnel for them to send home to their families and loved ones. He also enjoyed cycling around the various army camps on Salisbury Plain and was a regular visitor to Lark Hill airfield. Through 1911 and 1912, Thomas captured the activities of the Air Battalion and the early days of the Royal Flying Corps, and the Bristol Flying School. He would print suitable images as postcards, which were then sold for 'tuppence' in Amesbury and up at the airfield.

Postcards were widely used as a quick messaging medium; they were, if you like, the equivalent of email today, as well as giving the general public access to images they might not have otherwise seen – Fuller was one of its better exponents. His style is readily recognisable. The content, composition and perfect exposure of his sharply focused images compares favourably to many other photographers working at that time, and his work is a key visual accompaniment today to written accounts in the dynamic field of early aviation. Thomas' business continued around Amesbury and Salisbury Plain for many years after the closure of Lark Hill. During the First World War, he joined the RFC and in 1917 was serving as an Air Mechanic at Farnborough when he married Harriet. Before the end of the war Fuller was transferred to the Labour Corps, with whom he served near Rouen in France. Thomas and Harriet had six children and lived out their lives in Amesbury until Thomas died in 1962 at Salisbury Hospital.

Tom Fuller
selling postcards
at Lark Hill.
(J. Fuller)

# THE AIR COMPANY

By October 1910, Lord Esher had read accounts of Dickson's successful flights at the Great Autumn Manoeuvres, and was receiving reports back from similar exercises that had been conducted in France and Germany, and realised the Committee for Imperial Defence (CID) had, on his prompting, made a terrible mistake in shunning aeroplanes. He wrote an impassioned letter to them saying, 'Britain must arm herself with a whole fleet of aeroplanes. Unless she did so, she would be in mortal peril and for this the Imperial Defence Committee would be rightly blamed'.[1]

Shortly afterwards the CID announced its intention to form an Aviation Corps. The £9,000 annual budget for aviation, which, up until that point, had been spent entirely on balloons and airships, was increased to over £70,000 and the War Office set about procuring aeroplanes to supplement their rather worthless holding, which readers will recall comprised solely of the Short-Wright Type A, donated by Charles Rolls, and Laycock's troublesome Blériot XII.

They announced their intention to purchase a Henri Farman Militaire and Paulhan biplane. The Farman Type Militaire was simply a standard Type III, with upper wing extensions and an additional third rudder fitted centrally between the tailplanes, in the manner of the Bristol Boxkites. The Farman, which cost £1,008 (plus £5 for a Stewart aneroid – probably to act as an altimeter, and £15 12*s* for an Elliott rev counter), was handed over at Châlons on 26 November 1910, and shipped to Farnborough. Assembly was completed in the Balloon Factory, and it was ready for its first flight in January 1911. The pilot was Capt. Charles J. Burke of the Royal Irish Regiment who had recently returned with his pilot certificate from the Farman School. On 7 January, Burke took the Farman up before landing beside the factory. Ten minutes later he took off again, but stalled and the biplane crashed to the ground and was completely wrecked. Capt. Burke survived, but his right foot was badly crushed in the impact. The aeroplane was rebuilt by the Balloon Factory, at a cost of £160, and ready for flight again in March 1911, when it was test-flown at Laffen's Plain by Burke and Geoffrey de Havilland. On 16 March, Mervyn O'Gorman issued the first ever certificate of

Air Battalion Farman F1. (*Flight*)

Fulton and Paulhan talking at St Cyr, 1912. (*Flight*)

airworthiness for the Farman, now designated F1. In June 1911 Burke flew the Farman to Lark Hill and remained its regular pilot.

The second purchase was a Paulhan pusher biplane. Frenchman Louis Paulhan was, like many of the constructors, a pioneering aviator who had won the London to Manchester air race – the first long distance event in Britain staged in April 1910. His own unconventional biplane caused a sensation when shown at the Salon de l'Aeronautique held at Paris in October 1910. Paulhan's agent in Britain was George Holt-Thomas, the journalist who had covered the Lark Hill Manoeuvres, and it has been suggested his persuasiveness was responsible for the War Office's choice. In December 1910, Capt. Fulton was chosen to travel to St Cyr in France, where he was to inspect and accept the machine. As an artillery man, Fulton's selection did not sit well with the senior officers in the Engineers, but at that time he was one of the very few serving officers, in any regiment, who was qualified as an aeroplane pilot. Fulton asked his friend Cockburn to travel with him to France. The machine was demonstrated on 31 December, and the War Office's tests concluded on 11 January 1911. The Paulhan was purchased for £1,200, and arrangements were made to ship it back to Farnborough.

It arrived at the Balloon Factory on 16 February, and it was clear that the Commandant, Sir Alexander Bannerman, was in no rush to unpack the machine, only conceding O'Gorman's request seven days later on the basis that he wished to make drawings of the aeroplane. It did not fly until May 1911, by which time it had been earmarked for experiments. That autumn it was handed over to the Army, but never flown. By the end of the year, O'Gorman had negotiated to take the Paulhan for reconstruction, which commenced in February 1912.

Mervyn O'Gorman and his assistant, Frederick Green, recruited a young designer who was one of Britain's most talented and versatile aviators, Geoffrey de Havilland. Together they formed a team that was as ambitious as it was innovative. It was clearly understood that, despite its name, the Government-owned Balloon Factory would not be allowed to construct its own aeroplanes, but existed to conduct experiments and trials to develop and improve any commercially acquired machines. O'Gorman's idea of improvement was the most liberal interpretation possible, with machines taken into the workshops only to re-emerge as totally different aeroplanes. The first such 'experiment' involved the Blériot XII when, as previously mentioned, the tractor monoplane was re-invented as the SE1, a pusher biplane. In 1911 another opportunity presented itself in the form of a Voisin biplane presented by The Duke of Westminster. The aeroplane had been bought by the Duke when he had aspirations of learning how to fly himself. But in May 1911 Wilfred Lloyd, the Duke's Private Secretary, wrote to the War Office asking if the 'Flying Brigade' would like to have it. The offer was accepted, but on delivery to Farnborough the machine was found to be in poor condition and rather obsolete. It disappeared into the Royal Aircraft Factory only to reappear six months later bearing de Havilland's unmistakable influence, as the BE1.

On 28 February 1911, Army Order 61 was issued, stating:

> With a view to meeting Army requirements consequent on recent developments in aerial science it has been decided to form an Air Battalion, to which will be entrusted the duty of creating a body of expert airmen organised in such a way as to facilitate the formation of units ready to take to the field. The training and instruction of men in handling kites, balloons and aeroplanes and other forms of aircraft will also dissolve on this Battalion.[2]

It was realised that the four rather motley aeroplanes it had on inventory would be insufficient to complete the experiments, trials and training work required, and consequently on 14 March 1911 an order was placed for six Bristol Boxkites, at a discounted price of £849 each, plus a further two airframes that would be placed in reserve or used for spares.

The Air Battalion of the Royal Engineers was formed from the Army School of Ballooning on 1 April 1911 under the command of Major Sir Alexander

Bannerman.[3] The battalion, initially comprised fourteen officers and one hundred and fifty-three rank and file, twenty-three warrant officers and NCOs, two buglers, four riding horses and thirty-two draught horses, who were split into a headquarters and two companies. No.1 Company operated the Army's airships and balloons, and hence became known as 'The Gas Company', whilst No.2 Company operated fixed-wing powered aircraft and became known as 'The Air Company', under the command of Capt. John Fulton. It was the first British military unit to operate heavier-than-air machines. The War Office decreed that officers wishing to join the Air Battalion should have 'good eyesight, medical fitness, ability to read maps and make field sketches, an immunity to sea sickness and a knowledge of foreign languages'.[4] Special consideration was also given to bachelors who were under the age of thirty and weighed less than 11 stone 7 pounds (73kgs). Pilots were expected to have obtained a Royal Aero Club certificate from a flying school at their own expense, the cost of which was reimbursed when they successfully qualified as a military pilot.[5]

Despite the personal expense involved, there were plenty of volunteers to join the new battalion as pilots; however, they had difficulty recruiting the other ranks it required as tradesmen. Bannerman decided he would require blacksmiths, carpenters, electricians, engine drivers, fitters & turners, draughtsman, tinsmiths, collar makers, photographers and clerks. Most if not all of those who initially joined had previously served with the Army's Balloon Sections, and were well versed in the maintenance of balloons, airships and kites. This served the Gas Company's needs, but they had little knowledge of maintaining aeroplanes, or operating them in the field. There was no formal training, however, personnel posted to Lark Hill were able to pick up most of the necessary skills and techniques from the BCAC mechanics working in the adjacent flying sheds.

On 4 April 1911 the newly appointed Under-Secretary of State at the War Office, Col Seely, faced questions in the House of Commons from Lord Rothschild, on aeroplane numbers. Seely informed Parliament, 'We have obtained or ordered a sufficient number for instructional and experimental purposes, and further orders will depend upon our experience with these machines'.[6] The first two Bristol Boxkites were expected to arrive at Lark Hill from Filton later that month, but a late decision to fit Renault engines to two of the machines delayed their delivery. On 2 May, Seely was again being quizzed, this time by the Conservative MP Mr G. Sandys who asked him how many Air Battalion officers held RAeCCs, and how many were now stationed on Salisbury Plain. Seely responded 'Two officers … hold pilot's certificates and four officers attached on probation also hold certificates. No portion of the air battalion is at present stationed on Salisbury Plain, but during this month some portion may be in camp there.'[7] Two weeks later, No.2 Company was dispatched to Lark Hill from Farnborough, in anticipation of delivery of the first Boxkites on 18 and 25 May. Those joining Fulton at Lark Hill were Capt. C.J. Burke, Capt. E.M. Maitland,[8] Capt. E.B. Loraine, Lieut D.G. Conner, Lieut B.H.

Barrington-Kennett, Lieut R.A. Cammell, Lieut G.B. Hynes, Lieut S.D. Massey, Lieut A.G. Fox and Lieut H.R.P. Reynolds.

As will be noted in Seely's comments above, the distinction between officers in the Royal Engineers and those from other regiments was marked. Officers from other regiments were designated 'Assistant Engineers' whilst serving with the Air Battalion, and were subject to a Royal Engineer chain of command.

> The Air Battalion, bringing one machine, has now arrived from Aldershot for training, and four machines have since been taken over from the Bristol Co. These have been erected by the Bristol Co.'s staff, the work being watched by members of the Air Corps for the purpose of instruction.[9]

As this report proves, the Boxkites arrived at Lark Hill on time and were moved into the only permanent structures on site, the corrugated iron sheds built by the War Office that had been sitting since 1910, waiting to be used. However, accommodation here for the officers and men was more rudimentary, comprising a tented camp erected on the site now occupied by the Larkhill Garrison Church. The Air Company Officers were occasionally allowed to use Bulford Hut Barracks when not required for other personnel, and it is understood that some started using The Bustard Inn, a nearby pub, as the unofficial Officers' Mess.

Facing an obvious reluctance to build permanent accommodation on the airfield, coupled with rumours that the artillery were aiming to reclaim the flying ground and remove the aeroplane sheds at the earliest opportunity, did not help the newly arrived Air Company personnel settle in.

Cammell's Blériot XXI at Aldershot. (Author's collection)

George Cockburn spent April and May 1911 at Eastchurch teaching the first naval pilots, but having completed this task he returned to Lark Hill in the early summer to meet the officers of No.2 Company. His first impression is recorded as follows:

> The machines were, with the exception of the Blériot, either Farmans or Bristol Boxkites . . . Lieut Barrington-Kennett had no experience on these, and Lieut Reynolds had no experience on anything. The experience of the remainder was not sufficient to admit of their acting as instructors, so Capt. Fulton got permission for me to carry on and take Barrington-Kennett and Reynolds in hand. This [flying over Salisbury Plain] was an easy business compared with Eastchurch – a three-mile straight with good landing all the way made the first flights an easy matter. There were no incidents, except in a joy-ride for Lieut Cammell, when his cap blew off and back into the propeller, causing a most tremendous noise which scared us badly, me particularly, as I didn't know the cause . . . Progress was good; every one was very keen, and the Air Battalion soon developed into quite respectable pilots without any accidents.[10]

With summer approaching, the nation was eagerly anticipating its first major air race (the so called London-Manchester race was truthfully a 'first to achieve' challenge sponsored by the *Daily Mail*). Lord Northcliffe, the paper's proprietor envisaged a head-to-head competition that would involve flight around the country. The selection of Lark Hill as one of the checkpoints on The Circuit of Britain, on the final leg from Exeter to Brooklands, demonstrates its significance in aviation at this time. The Air Battalion's Lieut Cammell and Lieut Reynolds had entered. Cammell, in his own Blériot XXI, and Reynolds in Maitland's Howard Wright biplane, joined BCAC staff who were busy at Lark Hill preparing five of the company's own machines for the event.

# CIRCUIT OF BRITAIN AIR RACE, 1911

Having sponsored the 185-mile 1910 London-Manchester Race in 1910, Lord Northcliffe noted far greater challenges were now being staged in France. After considering either a London-Paris, or a London-Edinburgh event, Lord Northcliffe proposed a 1,010-mile Circuit of Britain Race that would be longer that any of the continental events and offered a prize of £10,000 to the pilot who could complete the fastest circuit. Although competitors would be airborne at the same time, it was a time trial, rather than a 'first across the line' event. The Royal Aeroclub was asked to organise the event, which started at Brooklands airfield and involved an anti-clockwise route, via Hendon, Edinburgh, and Bristol, then back to Brooklands, via thirteen compulsory checkpoints.

For most members of the British public this would likely be their first chance to see a flying machine. The event was not only a supreme test of endurance and piloting skills but designed by the RAeC to test the machine's reliability. Five essential parts on each competitor's airframe were marked with a seal and a further five engine parts similarly tagged; the rules stated that competitors had to finish with at least two parts from each set in place.

The 1911 *Daily Mail* Circuit of Britain Air Race map. (Author)

Thirty entries were received,[1] but only twenty-one aeroplanes reached Brooklands for the start on 22 July 1911. Among them was Samuel Cody flying the third version of his biplane. Since losing his position at the Balloon Factory, Cody had been allowed to continue his experiments on Laffen's Plain as a private experimenter. British Army Aeroplane No.1 had been modified and rebuilt several times but understandably, when you consider the treatment he had been given, the name linking it to the War Office had been dropped. Since its appearance at the Doncaster airshow in 1909, the machine had acquired the nickname 'The Flying Cathedral', and this was applied to all Cody's machines and their subsequent incarnations.

Three origins for the name have been suggested. Firstly, the towering balloon sheds at Farnborough, where he constructed his aeroplanes, resembled a cathedral knave and were often referred to as the Cathedral Sheds. Secondly, all of Cody's aeroplanes were massive by comparison with others machines (although it should be noted that each successive aeroplane Cody built was a little smaller than the last). Finally and, in this writer's mind, probably the true origin of the name, is thought to stem from the fact its upper and lower wings were not parallel, instead the lower wing tipped slightly downwards. The French term for such an arrangement was 'Katahedral' and it is not beyond the realms of imagination to see that the nickname could have stemmed from this mispronunciation. Certainly, Cody's team responded to this nickname and thereafter identified the various machines with the names of famous cathedrals, e.g. St Paul's.

First away from Brooklands at 3.00 p.m. was the Blériot of André Beaumont. The Frenchman, who had won the Circuit of Europe and other races that year, held a commission in the French Navy under his real name Lieut Jean Conneau (it appears common practice that serving officers would qualify to fly under a pseudonym). Following him was fellow Frenchman, Jules Védrines. Having spent six months working as Robert Loraine's mechanic in Britain during 1910, Védrines might have been reunited with his previous employer, as Loraine had also entered the race but was forced to withdraw before the start.

Cody III – The Circuit of Britain biplane outside his shed at Farnborough. (Author's collection)

Conneau and Védrines taking tea at Hendon. (*Flight*)

From the outset, Beaumont was able to put his naval training to good use and was a much better navigator than Védrines, however, the latter flew a faster aeroplane and had beaten Beaumont a number of times by the simple expedient of following Beaumont at a discrete distance and then, when the finish was in sight, accelerating to pass the Blériot and cross the line first. The BCAC team of Collyns Pizey, Howard Pixton and Gordon England suffered a setback when the latter's engine lost power and was unable to start. The last of nineteen starters got away for the short first leg to Hendon early that evening.

There was no flying on Sunday, and so on Monday morning an estimated 500,000 people turned out at 4.00 a.m. at Hendon, to see the first fliers take-off for Edinburgh. The 343-mile leg north into Scotland was hampered by fog, but Beaumont Blériot and his countryman Védrines' Morane-Borel were the first to arrive at the Harrogate control, where a further 150,000 spectators were waiting. The two pilots were airborne again for Newcastle within the hour. However, nine of their fellow competitors were not so lucky, including Lieut Cammell who, having been delayed on departure from Hendon, had to retire when forced down near Wakefield after the engine on his Blériot blew a cylinder.

Henry Astley's Birdling monoplane (a British-built copy of a Blériot) got as far as Kettering, where the pilot decided to stay overnight, but retired the following morning with faulty exhaust valves. Cody had an eventful trip to Harrogate; he had suffered a burst radiator pipe whilst passing Rotherham and a leaking fuel tank. These repairs necessitated an overnight stop in Yorkshire. This unexpected stopover allowed a spruce-looking Cody the opportunity to mingle with the crowds. The following morning, Cody departed early at 5.00 a.m., but his race almost came to an end at Newcastle. Outside of Durham he entered heavy fog and was unable to find the landing ground. 'For twenty terrifying minutes, he groped his way in the yellow mist, flying low over the town, zigzagging around chimney-stacks, church spires, flagpoles and high buildings. And missing some only by a few feet...'.[2] He eventually spotted some open ground and touched down outside Brandon

Hill Colliery in Durham, 17 miles short of his destination. Having chatted with some miners, he regained his bearings and Cody prepared to take-off again, but the aeroplane struggled to gain flying speed on the boggy field. Its undercarriage snagged on some barbed wire at the end of the field and the machine ran into a brick wall. The starboard wing was damaged. He telegraphed for replacement parts, and sent a message ahead to the next control point saying, 'Landed Near Durham Stop. Damaged Wing Stop. Hope To Arrive Wednesday Message Ends.' Harry Harper, who was covering the race, noted that, unlike the French manufacturers who were supported by teams of engineers, Cody was virtually a one-man effort (his two sons were valiantly trying to follow their father's progress by car). A colleague from *The Times* added, 'He carried all his tools in his pocket, and when the machine required repair, he came down and tinkered it himself with such material as he carried, or that could be procured from the local blacksmith.'[3]

Whilst effecting his repairs, news reached Cody that Beaumont had finished the race and been declared the winner. Cody realised the various delays he had experienced meant he could not complete the race within the time limit. Such was his spirit, however, that he was determined to continue, remarking 'I meant to do the course, even if I took a year over it'. Making the most of any delays, he arranged impromptu talks on his life, the race or anything else that might attract an audience.

Other competitors were having their share of problems too. Gustav Hamel, the German-born British pilot and Blériot's Chief Instructor at Hendon, was ahead of both Beaumont and Védrines until a broken inlet valve forced him to land at Melton Mowbray. Although he was not carrying spares, he was able to borrow a couple of valves from another pilot who had landed nearby. After four hours working on the engine, Hamel took off for Harrogate. After a brief rest there, he departed to the north but got lost in mist and, whilst landing to check his position, broke two bracing wires. Undaunted, he borrowed a car and drove onto Newcastle, where he collected his mechanics and returned to make repairs. After Newcastle he made two

Gordon England Bristol Challenger T-Type departs from Brooklands. (Author's collection)

The French pilot Védrines had once worked for Robert Loraine as a mechanic. (*Flight*)

further unexpected landings before reaching Edinburgh, the first at Innerwick, on the Firth of Forth, was due to strong winds, whilst the second was at East Linton, due to further engine trouble. He eventually arrived at his destination at 8.00 p.m. The following morning, Hamel departed for Stirling at 3.38 a.m., and then landed at Clarkson for repairs before making it to Glasgow around noon. Departing again for Carlisle he was forced to land at Thornhill, near Dumfries, where his father, who was providing ground support and no doubt getting worried about the number of mishaps, persuaded his son to retire from the race.

In the final stages of Beaumont's race he had been vying with Védrines and took the lead whilst en route to Bristol. On Wednesday 26 July the two pilots departed, hoping to complete the final leg in one day. The route would take them from Bristol southwest to Whipton, near Exeter, then east to Lark Hill and over to Brighton before the final stretch back to Brooklands. The *Flying Post* wrote,

A large crowd of several thousand gathered at Exeter on the evening of the 25th July, as the first competitors were expected before nightfall. However, no aircraft appeared in the sky, and the crowd dispersed, or camped out, ready for the expected arrival at 4 a.m. the next day. Special trains and trams were laid on and many returned before dawn, and there was an expectant excitement among the estimated ten to fifteen thousand spectators. Several times it was thought that the leading flyer was approaching the field, only for disappointment to run through the crowd. Then, shortly after 6 a.m., a speck was seen in the sky, followed by a second over Pinhoe Church . . . the spectators had had one of the finest sights of the whole circuit – two planes high in the air, within a quarter of a mile of each other, sailing along a third of a mile above the earth as serenely as a pair of seagulls.

Cheering burst out as the first aircraft approached at 1,500ft, then dropped down and landed. Védrines was the first to land followed two minutes later by Beaumont (who was still ahead of Védrines in the competition overall). The *Flying Post* continued, 'Védrines was obviously worried, and said little; Beaumont was affable and all smiles.' Védrines had lost time the day before because he had landed in the wrong field at Bristol, but effected a quick turn-around and was airborne again just thirty-eight minutes after landing at Whipton – Beaumont followed him eighteen minutes later.

When describing the conditions on the final day, Beaumont says,

Exeter–Salisbury Plain – flat, denuded country, lacking features. Weather very calm. At the splendid Salisbury military aviation field, I recover my cap, which I lost at Brooklands. An officer returned it to me. Full of joy, I assist in servicing the machine. They have already almost refilled the petrol tank. Suspecting that yesterday's petrol was impure, I make them empty it. I note that one of the fuel leads contains a great deal of castor oil! My trouble with the engine yesterday are explained all too easily. We clean out for three quarters of an hour.[4]

The scene at Lark Hill greeting Beaumont was described in *Flight* the following week:

The expected arrival of the competitors in the Daily Mail Circuit of Britain on Tuesday and Wednesday of last week caused the plain to be invaded by a large crowd of people, and on Tuesday it was estimated that the number present was between 2,000 and 3,000. In the morning, Mr Fleming gave several exhibition flights in his Bristol biplane, and his sharp turns, switchbacking and *vol planés* with both hands off the lever evoked loud applause . . . A large proportion of the crowd spent the night on the Plain, and members of the Bristol School were out the next morning at 3 a.m. giving exhibition flights. Up to 6 o'clock, M. Jullerot was giving lessons to pupils, and then took up the *Daily Mail* correspondent with a view to looking for 'Beaumont' and Védrines. After circling the Plains for an hour at a height of 2,000ft, during which time Védrines had landed, 'Beaumont' was sighted. They at once headed off to meet him, and came down at half-past eight.[5]

Védrines had, in fact, been sighted and escorted into Lark Hill by Henry Fleming flying another Bristol aeroplane. Cody did not arrive at Lark Hill until several days later, having been delayed by bad weather.

Although Védrines managed to catch up a little time on Beaumont, the latter arriving at Brooklands with a 1 hour 8 minutes 59 seconds lead. He had flown the 1,010 miles in a total time of 23 hours 38 minutes 3 seconds, at an average speed of 42.85mph. Lord Northcliffe was at the finish to welcome the victor, and subsequently presided at a luncheon at the Savoy Hotel when he presented Beaumont with a cheque for £10,000. The French naval officer had enjoyed a good summer as only a few weeks beforehand he won the Circuit of Europe race. His compatriot, Védrines, received a rather paltry consolation prize of £200. Samuel Cody completed the race in fourth place behind Jimmy Valentine, arriving at Brooklands ten days after the leader.

Summing up the event, *Flight* magazine commented,

It is now almost a matter of ancient history – how Beaumont won the great Circuit of Britain race in the air, with Védrines hard on his heels the whole way round. Much ink has been shed in illuminating the personalities of the two men, and in the glorification of their wonderful pluck and endurance, with the result that both of them are probably better known to the man in the street than many of those who direct the fortunes of empires . . . we are dead against the modern disposition to lionise all and sundry, with or without excuse; but this race of the air is one of those occasions on which it is more than justifiable to make heroes of men. As it was, the whole kingdom went flying mad, to use the popular term, during the days when the interest of the race was at its height . . . in the streets, in the clubs, in public conveyances, there was but the one topic of conversation – the great race. It must have driven home the main fact that a new era has arrived in which the last remaining element has been almost mastered by the genius of man, and have set people speculating very seriously upon its true significance.[6]

Shortly after the race, Claude Grahame-White arranged a benefit meeting at Hendon airfield to compensate Védrines for losing by such a small margin. Both Beaumont and Grahame-White flew despite strong winds on the day, and over fifty thousand spectators turned out to give Védrines a vociferous welcome and raised more than £2,000 from admissions and donations.

Both Cody and Valentine completed the circuit outside the allotted timescale, and received nothing for their efforts. In order to earn something to cover his expenses, Cody remained at Brooklands over the Bank Holiday weekend intending to fly some demonstrations and compete for the Manville prize (awarded for the longest aggregate flying time over a specified number of days). By Monday, the last day of the contest, Cody had established a good total and was comfortably in the lead. His main competitor was Howard Pixton, who was having difficulty accumulating time as his machine's engine was prone to overheating and he could only remain airborne for a few minutes at a time. Late in the afternoon, Cody departed for home, feeling confident he had done enough to win the £500 prize; however, as the temperature dropped that evening Pixton was able to take off and log enough time to take the lead, and subsequently he won the prize.

In the aftermath of the Circuit of Britain, BCAC were in contention with the Royal Aero Club with regards to the banning of their pilot Graham-Gilmore from entering the race. The club had suspended his flying certificate on account of several alleged misdemeanours, including low flying over the Henley regatta. BCAC claimed that they had spent a considerable amount of money on the entry and the ban, imposed a few days before the race was due to start, gave them no time to find a replacement pilot. The RAeC had clearly changed its attitude and was starting to exercise its muscles. According to Frank McClean, the club had become 'more hard-bitten with the advent of mechanisation'. He would much later recall, 'The Aero Club Members in the years before 1909 were a quiet, sedate, genteel body whose only vice was to be considered by the hoi-polloi as amiable lunatics. They consisted of city gentlemen, lawyers, wine merchants,

Advertisement for Bristol Flying School, showing the company's commitment to training Army officers. (*Flight*)

THE BRITISH AND COLONIAL
AEROPLANE CO., LTD.

Head Offices: Clare Street House, Bristol, England.

# Army Air Battalion.

The attention of Officers of His Majesty's
Army is especially directed to our offer of

## SPECIAL TERMS AND FACILITIES

for qualifying for the newly formed

Air Battalion

## Flying Schools,

### Salisbury Plain,

*adjoining the Great Military Camp,*

## and Brooklands.

The celebrated "Bristol" Military Biplanes are
provided for the use of Officers.

### STAND No. 47, OLYMPIA.

WRITE FOR PARTICULARS AND TERMS.

Peers of the Realm and their offspring, and they dined together once a month at Jules' in Jermyn Street.'[7] But now they had assumed the position of regulator, and the officers of the club were taking this responsibility seriously. On 21 July the Graham-Gilmore case appeared before the court of appeal. BCAC claimed that the club had no right to suspend a certificate that had not been issued by them (Gilmour had a certificate awarded by the Aéro-Club de France). The RAeC defended its position, stating it was empowered to do so by the International Aeronautical Federation, and that in their opinion Graham-Gilmore's flights were dangerous and contrary to regulations. The court decision was that the club had acted properly for the protection of the public, but also criticised them for not allowing Graham-Gilmore sufficient opportunity to defend himself against the accusation.

# DEVELOPMENTS WITHIN BCAC

After just one year of production, BCAC had registered seventy-six Boxkites either as newly built airframes, or machines that had been re-registered after a major rebuild or modification;[1] however, the company directors were fully aware that their design was being eclipsed by faster and lighter monoplanes. In the summer of 1911, Bannerman, Commandant of the Air Battalion, wrote to the War Office saying,

> It must be recognised that (Boxkites) do not fulfil all the conditions required of military aeroplanes. As beginners' machines they are admirable, and none could have served better to allow the Air Battalion getting experience in flying, but they do not have the speed necessary to allow aeroplanes to fly in any but the finest weather, and the Air Battalion pilots now possess the experience [for] a more advanced type.[2]

Earlier that year, BCAC had asked Challenger and Pizey to create within the company an experimental, or X, department, and the two men were sent to Lark Hill to learn to fly under the guidance of M. Tetard. When they were ready, George Cockburn observed them as they flew the test required for their RAeC certificates. However, during training Pizey had shown such aptitude for flying that he was asked to remain at Lark Hill as a Flying School instructor, and he was later appointed as the school's manager.

Pizey's place in the team at Filton was taken by Archibald Low, and together

Collyns Pizey became manager of the Bristol Flying School. (*Flight*)

Challenger and Low produced designs for a monoplane and a small biplane that was tested at Lark Hill in February. The monoplane needed further development, but both machines went on display at the 1911 Olympia Aero Show. Around this time Challenger left BCAC and joined the French Esnault-Pelterie Company, where he continued to develop the monoplane design. Leon Versepuy took over the monoplane flight tests, but could not get off the ground and this particular monoplane was abandoned in anticipation of the arrival of Pierre Prier, who had been brought in as Challenger's replacement. Not much is known about Versepuy, however, in June 1911 he took one of the military Boxkites from Lark Hill over the channel and demonstrated it at various venues across France.

Pierre Prier started with BCAC in June 1911. An accomplished engineer, he was also a qualified pilot and had been Blériot's Chief Flying Instructor at Hendon. The previous year, Prier had taught Frank Hedges Butler how to fly an aeroplane, the balloon pioneer deciding to try his hand at powered aviation. Having Prier on the workforce was seen as quite a coup at BCAC, and they asked him to design a racing monoplane so they could compete in the Gordon Bennett Cup Race taking place at Eastchurch in July. This was too much to ask for, and the machine was not completed in time, so Prier turned his attention towards developing the Challenger design ready for the Circuit of Britain race. Prier completed his prototype and it was tested at Lark Hill in the summer of 1911.

> The new Bristol monoplane was brought out for the first time, and, with M. Prier in charge, made a very fine flight of 55 minutess, during which a height of over 1,600ft was reached. M. Prier made a beautiful landing by means of a *vol plané*, and explained that he had only come down owing to the petrol supply getting very low. The machine behaved very well, and appeared to be extremely fast.[3]

It was not well received, with Capt. Fulton commenting that the machine was completely unsuitable in its present state of development. However, this condemnation did not stop the War Office purchasing one for £850, and it was presented to the Air Battalion on 17 February 1912. Perhaps unsurprisingly it did not fly for a month, and only then for a brief hop. Lieut Reynolds, the pilot for that first flight, took the Prier up again at the end of April but crashed and the monoplane had to be returned to Filton for repair.

Further development of the Prier continued, with Bertram Dickson contributing to the design, suggesting improvements to the tail controls. The first so-called Prier Dickson monoplane appeared in August 1912, when it was flown by Capt. Allen, and a second followed in September just before the ban on monoplane flying was declared (see Chapter 20). Thirty-four Prier monoplanes were built in all; they were sold to the War Office, and exported to Italy, Spain, Germany and Turkey. Pierre Prier remained at BCAC for just twelve months, and when he departed another brilliant designer, Henri Coanda, replaced him.

# BACK ON MANOEUVRES

With the Air Battalion split between its two sites at Farnborough and Lark Hill, debate arose as to the merits of each. There was a shortage of aeroplane storage on Laffen's Plain at the former, and although the flying ground had been cleared to some degree, it was still rough and uneven with too many trees on and around the perimeter. Laffen's Plain was still common land, with open access to the public who were frequently encountered walking their dogs there.

Capt. Fulton wrote in favour of Lark Hill claiming that in his opinion Farnborough was both dangerous and unsuitable for operating the newer and faster aeroplanes to which the Air Battalion aspired. However, Maj. Bannerman was unhappy with the remoteness of Salisbury Plain, and concerned it would engender slack attitudes among his men. So he recalled most of them to Farnborough, suggesting, 'I think it advisable to recall [No.2 Company] . . . in order that the men may live in barracks, do a little drill, and generally smarten up.'[1] A small cadre of military aviators remained at Lark Hill, consisting of Fulton, Burke, Cammell, Reynolds, Barrington-Kennett and Connor, who were supported by a team of three mechanics. Despite the size of the team, these men were beginning to find a niche for themselves, undertaking experimental and trial work, and in the process they set a number of

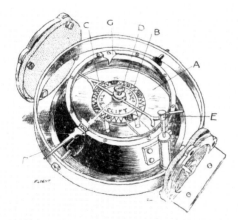

THE NEW CLIFT COMPASS.—A. Transparent container. B Compass card. C. Course pointer. D. Adjusting screw. E. Clamping screw. F. Fixed lubber point. G. Adjustable lubber point.

The Clift compass was fitted to military Boxkites. (*Flight*)

Salisbury Plain – Big sky countryside. (Author)

1909 Grande Semaine de Aviation at Rheims. (Unknown)

British & Colonial Aeroplane Co. Ltd logo on a propeller. (Author's collection)

BCAC sheds at Lark Hill, 2011. (Author's collection)

The Bake, 2012 – Dickson's landing site. (Author's collection)

Receipt for flying training. (Unknown)

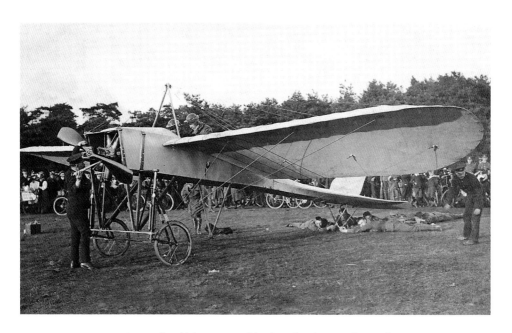

Cammell's Blériot XXI at Aldershot. (Author's collection)

Circuit of Britain Air race 1910 programme. (Unknown)

Lark Hill flying ground, 2012. (Author's collection)

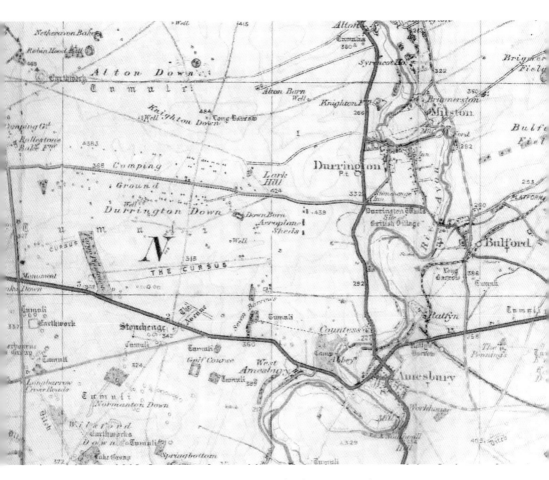

Durrington Down, 1913. (Ordnance Survey)

Lark Hill. (Ordnance Survey)

aviation records. Lieut Cammell's Blériot XXI was used to test a 100ft long-trailing wireless aerial, the Dines air-speed indicator, the Baird altimeter and Heath & Clift compass, which he suspended in the cockpit on chains in an attempt to eliminate unwanted vibrations, and that allowed him to experiment with 'blind flying' through fog. Using only the compass and a clinometer, he described the experience as 'successful, but rather alarming in gusts'. During July 1911, Cammell flew several sorties during cavalry manoeuvres to assess the accuracy of dropping messages attached to streamers, from aeroplanes to troops on the ground; and to assess the clarity with which pilots could see instructions laid out by those troops from the air.

One year after Dickson and the Boxkites had performed so admirably at Lark Hill, the 1911 round of manoeuvres was planned to take place in training areas in Cambridgeshire. The Air Battalion was tasked to support them, which would involve the furthest group deployment they had yet attempted. The Air Company planned to base themselves at two locations, Snarehill Farm, near Thetford, and Hardwicke Farm, near Cambridge. When news came through that the manoeuvres had been cancelled, Major Bannerman decided the Air Company should continue with its plans, as it would provide good training. Capt. Fulton's log gives us an insight into the problems the newly formed unit faced during the deployment. One of their number in particular, Lieut Reynolds, was to survive a most remarkable adventure; the retelling of which would undoubtedly enlighten many a subsequent evening at the officers' mess, and no doubt the bars in Amesbury.

Reynolds departed Lark Hill on Wednesday 16 August. He got as far as Oxford without incident. He intended to remain there for a few days, for reasons unknown, and departed on Saturday for Cambridge, with a planned short stop at Launton near Bicester. The possibility of thunderstorms seemed remote, but as he was approaching Bletchley he noted the air had become steadily bumpier. When a large black cumulonimbus cloud loomed up on his starboard bow, Reynolds decided it prudent he should land. Flying at a height of around 1,700ft he switched off his engine and pointed Boxkite No. F7 towards the ground, but a sudden, violent gust caught the tail, and the elevator, which was fixed on booms in front of the aircraft, swung down beyond the perpendicular. As Reynolds was not strapped in he was thrown from his seat and had no clear recollection of the following few seconds. He later suggested, 'I suppose I caught hold of the uprights at my side . . . for the next thing I realised was that I was lying in a heap on what was normally the under-surface of the top plane [wing]. The machine was in fact upside-down.'[2] As the aircraft flipped and swung from side-to-side, falling like a leaf, Reynolds struggled to his feet and held tightly onto the struts between the two wings. At one point, the swinging stopped and the aeroplane fell sideways. Reynolds could do nothing now, as unlike balloon crews, aeroplane pilots did not carry parachutes. He hung on, and as his luggage fell to earth, tightened his grip expecting that any moment he might follow. As the ground got rapidly closer the

Lieut Herbert Reynolds. (*Flight*)

swinging motion started again. Somehow he retained the presence of mind to realise his survival depended on the aeroplane hitting the ground mid-swing, when it would be moving comparatively slowly.

The final oscillation started about 30ft (10m) above the ground and the aeroplane slid sideways towards the ground once more. According to witnesses Reynolds jumped clear from a height of about 10ft. He later said, 'Something hit me on the head and scratched it slightly, but what it was I did not know, for I was in too much of a hurry to get away from the machine to inquire.'[3] Reynolds fell to the ground and lay there to regain his composure. Two men who had been swimming naked in a nearby river had seen the alarming descent, and they ran to the scene without considering their state of undress. Reynolds opened his eyes, saw the two naked men standing over him, and closed his eyes again quickly. Local villagers began to arrive, and thought the two men must be crew from the wrecked aeroplane, whose clothes had been torn off in the accident. During the subsequent and hilarious misunderstandings, Reynolds lay still on the ground, with his eyes closed, until the commotion had died down.[4]

Five aircraft set out from Lark Hill for Cambridge. Lieut Connor (in Boxkite F5), navigating with a makeshift map he had torn from *Bradshaw's Railway Guide*, crashed on high ground in fog; Massey's aeroplane suffered an engine failure. It was repaired in the field but he crashed it again when attempting to take off.

Meanwhile, Brooke-Popham and Burke's Farman (F1) damaged a tail-skid whilst landing at Burcott. Only Lieut Barrington-Kennett (F8) and Lieut Cammell (who followed the others in his own Blériot several days later) reached their destination unscathed. Where they 'passed several days… entertained by the dons at the nearby university'.[5] But regrettably, on the return flight, Cammell added to the list of damaged machines. *Flight* reported that whilst he was attempting to land downwind at

Capt. John Fulton in his Blériot XI. (*Flight*)

Hendon 'Lieut Cammell charged the doors of a hangar ... at 30mph, after touching his Blériot down more than 200yds away. He was assisted by a strong following wind. Fortunately, the doors gave way.'[6]

The effort to repair or recover the battalion's damaged aircraft, which were now scattered across the south of England, was considerable. Every evening for the next four days, beacons were lit at Lark Hill to guide home the members of the Air Company safely back to Salisbury Plain. Capt. Fulton's diary, copied verbatim, gives a good account of this eventful deployment:

# 15–26 August 1911

## *First Installment*

**Tues 15.** Lark Hill. Burke (F1) left in the evening for Oxford, with Brooke-Popham passenger. Alighted at Hungerford.

**Wed 16.** Lark Hill. BK (Barrington-Kennett), Massy, Reynolds, Connor left in evening for Oxford. BK alighted Uffington with broken tailskid. Hynes left at 10 PM in WD car with a spare tailskid for him. Massy and Reynolds reached Oxford. Connor reached Kintbury undamged with F5.

**Thur 17.** BK continued to Wantage: and then to Oxford. Massy remained at Oxford. Reynolds & Burke ditto. Conner left Kintbury & alighted at West Isley in fog, damaged top and bottom main planes. Hynes returned to Larkhill (from Uffington) at 11.30 a.m. and left again in WD car with breakdown trolley at 2.30 p.m. to go to Conner at W.Isley. Hynes reach W.Isley and found machine about 7.15 p.m.; left trolley there to be loaded and went to Oxford arriving at 10 p.m. Conner remained with F5 machine. Burke telegraphed me (in answer to my enquiry) that he had been unable to leave Oxford, as he could not buy any maps in Oxford.

**Fri 18.** BK, Burke, Reynolds & Massy all at Oxford. Conner returned to Lark Hill by rail at 4.30 p.m. and tested spare machine. Hynes went from Oxford to W.Isley and brought in part of F3 to Port Meadow.

**Sat 19.** BK, Burke, Reynolds and Massy all left Oxford in foggy weather. Burke alighted Burcot with broken tailskid. Massy down at Marsh-Gibbon, undamaged, engine trouble. BK down at Marsh-Gibbon undamaged: got engine changed for F3s engine which was taken to him from Port Meadow in hired car. Reynolds down at Launton, undamaged. WD car went to Farnborough to get tailskid for Burke. WD car returned 3 p.m. and took tailskid to Burke, but found he had gone. Reynolds left Launton and smashed at Simpson. Massy smashed in starting from Marsh-Gibbon. BK got to Apsley Guide undamaged. Burke got to Grendon Underwood and smashed tailplane: he wired to Cammell to send him spare tailplanes from his shed at Lark Hill. Conner left Lark Hill 5 a.m. in fog and alighted Port Meadow Oxford at 6.40 a.m. Snapped wires during *vol plane* descent, breaking propeller in mid-air. F9 stored in Oxford aerodrome. Fulton drove his car to Oxford, taking Wilson and Cullen.

**Sun 20.** BK reached Blunham in morning undamaged. Burke still at Grendon Underwood. Fulton visited Burke and Massy, taking their tools and full detachments to each. Hynes fitted new tyre to trolley and did transport work all morning; went to W. Isley with trolley in afternoon and brought in rest of F5. All F5 now stored in Oxford aerodrome. Major Sir A. Bannerman visited Oxford with instructions for Fulton: he then visited Reynolds at Simpson, taking Ridd with him. Wyners-Stewart arrived to replace Hynes on breakdown work: Hynes having orders to go to Breguet's works. Tailplanes arrived Oxford by hired car from Lark Hill. Fulton drove own car to Grendon Underwood again, taking tailplanes to Burke. Burke said he was not satisfied with them. Fulton then drove to Massy at Marsh-Gibbon and arranged to send trolley to take his machine on to Hardwicke camp. Sent note to Cammell at Lark Hill by hired car which brought Burke's tailplanes from there, to ask him to send spares for repairs of Massy's Bristol.

**Mon 21.** Sapper Spencer arrived by train with the spares, which I yesterday asked Cammell to send for Massy's Bristol, but find that Cammell has sent Farman spares instead of Bristol! Stewart left early with trolley to load up Massy's F7 and take him to Hardwicke camp. BK left Blunham and alighted Biggleswade uninjured. He continued in evening and reached Hardwicke camp safely. Wired him not to go beyond Hardwicke. Sent Vagg and Arvoye's bits to Cambridge. Sent Wyners-Stewart's kit to Cambridge. Breakdown trolley reached Massy to be loaded. Stewart went on to Hardwicke in WD car in WD car with Massy's engine. Sent Reynolds detachment by rail to Simpson. Met Brooke-Popham accidentally in Oxford railway station saying he was going off to Farnborough to arrange the matter of tailplanes. He has left machine in open with orders to detachment not to carry our repairs. Sent Burkes detachment bits to them. Sent Spencer to Hardwicke (Reason: fear that the stores for the two camps have got mixed at Lark Hill)

**Tues 22.** Farnborough wires manoeuvres abandoned. Wired them my proposals for return of machines to Lark Hill. No news of Burke, who is presumably still at Farnborough. Visited Burke's machine at Grendon Underwood to try and get news of Burke. Took Wilson with me, who inspected Burke's engine, ran it and found it satisfactory. Awaiting orders re. my proposals.

**Wed 23.** Visited Burke: found he had returned and was beginning repairs at last with parts which I supplied him. Total delay in commencing repairs to this machine (F1) since necessary parts reached Burke on Sun. afternoon last: 62 hours. Brought back de Havilland in my car, whom Burke had brought with him from Farnborough. Sent Thomas's kit and Massy's revolution counter to Hardwicke by train. Sent Geard and Langton to Hardwicke by rail.

## Second Installment

**Wed 23.** Visited Burke in own car, twice, taking him tools etc. and bringing back de Havilland, whom he had there with him. Dispatched Geard and Langton by train to BK at Hardwicke. Dispatched Thomas's kit and speed indicator ditto.

**Thurs 24.** Sent detailed orders to Hardwicke and Thetford regarding breaking up of camps. Wire came from Hardwicke to say that Burke was asking for petrol and oil. Suppose that Burke has started and landed somewhere, as he did not ask me for petrol and oil on either of the four occasions on which I have visited him by motor car from Oxford, and I cannot otherwise understand why he should wire Hardwicke (80 miles away) rather than Oxford (17 miles). Wired massy to let me know where Burke is. Wired back "Burke is at Grendon-Underwood". So at 10 p.m. went to the aerodrome at Oxford and knocked up the man in charge. Succeeded in getting 14 gall of petrol and 5 gall of castor oil, as supposed for some reason. Burke had had to empty his tanks. Drove onto Grendon: Burke not there: supposed to be at Marsh-Gibbon. Eventually found Burke, who said he did not require oil or petrol. Could not understand his explanation of the reason he had wired for it. Drove back to Oxford with oil and petrol.

**Fri 25.** Letter from Massy at Hardwicke to say Carden not there. Decided to go immediately in own motor to Hardwicke. Burke came to me at Oxford by train to say he had smashed at Grendon on starting. Sent him to Farnborough to get spares, as he says he wants to fly his own machine back. This was against my advice, which is to dismantle it and return it by road or rail. Went to Hardwicke in own car to make arrangements there for getting machines away and closing camp. Settle everything there.

**Sat 26.** At Hardwicke Cammell arrived at 6.30 a.m. on Blériot. Returned to Oxford in own car. Four main planes arrived for F5: as factory spares different to Bristol spares. Decided too big a task to completely rebuild F5 so far from home, so ordered F5 to be packed into truck with the four spare main frames and all sent to Lark Hill.

J.D.B. Fulton. Capt.[7]

# 13

# A RACE TO THE DEATH

In 1911, the governments of Europe were involved in arms races, and struggles that signposted the inevitability of conflict. At the start of the twentieth century Britain firmly believed in the importance of naval supremacy, and it was accepted Government policy that the size of the Royal Navy should equate to the combined strength of the next two largest navies in the world. However, Germany had aspirations of naval supremacy and was building Dreadnought-style battleships as fast as they could, resulting in a classic arms escalation situation. Relations between France and Germany were further strained in July 1911, when the latter sent a gunboat to Agadir in North Africa to defend, or so they claimed, a German colony. This was seen as a challenge to the French Government's attempt to establish a protectorate in a country in which they had had interests for over 100 years. The event, which also involved Britain and Spain, became known as the 'Morocco Crisis'. David Lloyd-George fired a warning shot at the Mansion House when he said, 'If Britain is treated badly where her interests are vitally affected ... then I say emphatically that peace at that price would be a humiliation intolerable for a great country like ours to endure.'[1] The German Government backed down, a reaction possibly triggered in part by a serious financial crisis, and the offer from France to trade some territorial rights in other parts of Africa, however, it was an uneasy truce and a deep suspicion remained among all concerned.

Westminster was anxious that the Air Battalion was not growing quickly enough to respond to any hostility that might develop from the tensions, and there were those who feared the procurement of foreign built aeroplanes for military work would restrict future employment of the Air Battalion, as it would be impossible to distinguish friendly and foreign aircraft during conflict (although, at this time, offensive operations were not a major objective for the Air Battalion). Responding to questions asked in parliament on these issues, Bannerman stated 'It is an open question whether the small results to be expected even from large charges, dropped more or less wildly [could] be taken to justify the risk of losing invaluable aircraft,' and he added 'if ever the time comes when the armaments of the Crown are divided into land forces, sea forces and air forces, the number of aircraft may be so great as to render offensive action feasible ... but that time is not yet.'[2]

Col Seely was challenged over War Office estimates that between eighty and one hundred officers would need to be trained as both pilot and observers if the country went to war, and whether this target was achievable. He admitted, 'Our present arrangements do not admit of opportunities for training so large a number, the Army Council is in communication with the various civilian schools of aviation in regard to the training of selected officers and the terms they would consider sufficient; and it is proposed to make a grant in aid of the expenses of such training.'[3] The shortage of aircrew was matched by a lamentably small number of aircraft; however, measures were in hand to improve that situation.

As stated previously, BCAC staff were testing Prier's monoplane design in the sheds at Lark Hill. Three versions were being produced; a single-seat and twin-seat machine, both fitted with a Gnome 50hp engine, and another twin-seater, fitted with a 35hp Anzani – the latter specifically intended for pupils who could not be expected to handle a monoplane at 65mph until well trained on machines of a more moderate speed. Horatio Barber and the Aeronautical Syndicate Limited had presented four Valkyrie monoplanes to the Government earlier that year. A seemingly generous gesture; however, on inspecting these machines, Lieut Samson RN assessed they were not in a good state of repair. Two of the machines were assigned to the Admiralty, and transported by road to the Naval Flying School at Eastchurch; meanwhile, Lieut Cammell was ordered to proceed to Hendon and take delivery of the remaining pair for the Army and fly them over to Farnborough. On Sunday, 17 September 1911 Cammell and a team of mechanics arrived at Hendon and set about replacing the engine in one machine with a 50hp Gnome unit they had brought along with them. With the engine change complete, Cammell took off at 5.40 p.m. to fly a few circuits to familiarise himself with the machine. During one of these circuits another aeroplane, possibly one flown by Gustav Hemel, arrived over the airfield. It is thought that in order to give way to that machine, Cammell put the Valkyrie into a steep turn at a height of less than 100ft, whereupon it started to sideslip and could not be recovered before crashing into the ground. Cammell was not wearing a crash helmet, and without the protection of a harness, was thrown from the wreckage and sustained serious head injuries. The twenty-five-year-old was taken to hospital but declared dead on arrival. The crash was witnessed by Barber and Cammell's colleague Capt. Eustace Loraine, who stated at the subsequent inquest that Cammell appeared to turn too tightly and may not have been familiar with the different flight controls fitted to the Valkyrie.[4] Cammell was buried four days later at Aldershot with full military honours. Sadly, it is now a matter of fact that the first British officer to perform his duty as a military aeroplane pilot was also the first to be killed in the course of those duties. In a short flying career, Cammell had achieved much. It is notably punctuated with numerous crashes and forced landings leading up to this fatal crash, however, his willing attitude and determination not to give up should not be overlooked. It is undeniable that he was involved in a number of incidents, but he was still at the cutting-edge of aviation – like many of his colleagues, flying by the seat of his pants and learning as he went along. Without such resolve, demonstrated over a period of little more than a year, and the trials he conducted, often on his own Blériot at his own personal expense, aviation might not have progressed at the rate it did. *Flight* stated that Cammell's death brought home to the public 'The heroic self-sacrifice of those Army and Naval officers who have voluntarily, and for the most part at their own expense, devoted themselves to perfecting aviation in the interests of national defence.'[5]

In the autumn of 1911, Capt. Fulton, with Capt. Sykes and Lieut Barrington-Kennett, travelled to Rheims to observe the French Military Trials. A total of forty-four aeroplanes and five airships took part in the competition to assess a suitable machine and the prospect of winning a top prize worth £30,000 (it would be another two years before Britain could come close to mustering such numbers of flying machines). Fulton returned home, and on 8 September 1911 wrote a memorandum to the War Office recommending they purchase for the Air Battalion a Breguet, a Nieuport, a Deperdussin and a Sommer aeroplane.

But it was not only the Air Battalion officers who were impressed by what they had seen in France. Mr Sandys MP attended and commented 'At the present time … there are only six officers of the Army Air Battalion actually engaged in flying, and unless there are very good grounds indeed for supposing that the military authorities of other countries are totally wrong, and have completely over-estimated the value of aeroplanes, we are running a very serious risk indeed.'[6] These cautious words, and the army officers' reports, were instrumental in the announcement of the following December, that Britain would stage their own trials at Lark Hill during 1912.[7]

Deperdussin at Lark Hill, probably in the shed originally built for Charles Rolls in 1910. (Author's collection)

Among Fulton's other recommendations was that the War Office should consider purchasing portable hangars, which were being produced by the Bessonneau Company at Vosges. These wooden and canvas structures would suit the expeditionary force, in that they were relatively mobile and could be erected by an unskilled workforce in around two days. The Bessonneau hangars were also available in two standard sizes and represented good value for money when the Government was trying to expand its aviation assets (500m² costing 12,000F and 400m² for 8,000F). A number of hangars were bought, and then subsequently produced in Britain by Ransom, Simms & Jeffries of Ipswich and other firms. Despite their temporary appearance a number were still in use on military airfields in Britain seventy years or so later. It is quite possible that the purchase and widespread use of Bessoneaus was responsible for the shift from the use of 'shed', which was quite inappropriate for these structures, to the adoption of the French word 'hangar', as the standard term for aeroplane storage.

By end of the year the Air Battalion had four new machines (three of which had been recommended by Fulton). Air Battalion officers were detailed off to travel to France and collect machines that had performed particularly well during the military trials. The first was a two-seat Nieuport IVG monoplane, which Barrington-Kennett 'adopted' as his personal machine. Lieut Hynes was sent to the Breguet School at Douai, where he was taught to fly a biplane, that Cockburn would later describe as 'A most unwholesome beast with flexible wings, steel spars and wheel control'.[8]

Meanwhile, Fulton claimed the two-seat Deperdussin for himself. Another of O'Gorman's adaptations arrived fresh from the Aircraft Factory at Farnborough. It was officially called the BE1 but became known as the 'Silent Army Aeroplane' owing to its engine being considerably quieter than the other machines. Lieut Burke chose this as his personal machine.

Lieut George Bayard Hynes in the unusual Breguet biplane. (*Flight*)

With these new machines on the inventory, there was a sense that the Army had started to use relatively modern aeroplanes, however, the fact that three of the four aeroplanes were French did not impress the British manufacturers. On 5 December, a group of representatives from these companies, including A.V. Roe, Handley Page, Horace Short, Claude Grahame-White, John Dunne, Bertram Dickson, as well as representatives of Vickers, the Royal Aero Club and the Aeronautical Society, met Col Seely. Dunne opened, calling for the government to make 'the establishment of an internal source of supply a priority'.[9] The recent announcement of an open military aeroplane competition (aka the military aircraft trials) to be held at Lark Hill had done little to appease the companies. Seely listened to their comments but neatly ducked the issue, pointing out that they would not be wise to rely too much on military orders, which could not possibly be sufficient to sustain an industry on the scale envisaged.[10]

Whilst debate raged over the flying machines in Whitehall that winter, the domestic arrangements at Lark Hill were alarming. With his men sometimes bedding besides their horses for warmth, Capt. Fulton wrote to the Battalion HQ, reporting that the condition of the sheds was deteriorating in the cold and damp, and as a consequence the aeroplanes were suffering. He informed Bannerman that wooden airframes were warping and metalwork rusting. In the freezing conditions engine bolts in the aeroplanes had crystallized and sheared off, and the laminated wooden propellers were splitting in the damp; Fulton requested a number of Carbotron wood stoves, which were quickly provided.

Not that the officers of the Air Battalion could do much to escape from the discomfort of Salisbury Plain, as, according to *The Pall Mall Gazette* in January 1912, they were now forbidden from flying cross-country other than 'ploughing a lonely furrow between Salisbury and Aldershot'.[11] Commenting on this announcement *Flight* informs its readers that 'flights further afield may entail expense in petrol and oil... and the funds of the Air Battalion do not admit such

The Silent Army Aeroplane - Geoffrey de Havilland's BE.1. (Author)

Engine repair workshops inside the Lark Hill sheds, note the wood-burning stove. (Unknown)

generous expenditure', adding the opinion that it was somewhat of a War Office tradition to ensure that the British Army was unprepared for any future conflict. The ban on cross-country flying does not appear to have been well heeded or to have reduced the desire to set new records; and on 14 February Lieut B.H. Barrington-Kennett, along with Cpl Ridd RE, took off from Lark Hill in a Nieuport Monoplane to attempt a new duration record. Four hours and thirty-two minutes later they accomplished their task, and, in addition to completing the longest flight, they broke the long-distance record, covering a distance of 249 miles and 840 yards around a small circuit marked out on Salisbury Plain. Later that summer, Barrington-Kennett was awarded the RFC Mortimer Singer prize of £500, and to express his gratitude took the men of the Air Battalion out to a celebratory dinner (a similar prize offered to the RNAS was won by Lieut Arthur Longmore RN, but he only accomplished a flight of 181 miles in three hours fifteen minutes). The 'work hard, play hard' ethos paid off and such achievements helped the men of the Air Company acquire a certain celebrity status. The pilots in particular were welcome guests at parties and gatherings across the country. It was commonplace for them to fly off to country houses for shooting and hunting weekends, where well-to-do families would entertain them, and it is said they were very popular with the wives and daughters. On at

Lieut Barrington-Kennett who won the Mortimer-Singer Prize in February 1912. (*Flight*)

least one occasion, Reynolds and Barrington-Kennett got into trouble for being away from Lark Hill for a whole week, ostensibly with mechanical problems.

## A Week on Salisbury Plain – As reported in *Flight*, 9 December 1911

**Air Battalion** – On Wednesday of last week the weather was ideal for flying, after the mist had cleared off in the early morning, and the Air Battalion was soon at work, five machines being brought out almost at once. The first to take to the air was Lieut Reynolds on a Bristol military biplane, followed by Lieut Barrington-Kennett who had arrived the previous day from France, where he had been learning to fly the Nieuport. He made a good trial on one of these monoplanes, and at the same time Lieut Hinds was up on the Breguet biplane, with and without passengers, one of those carried being Staff Sergeant Wilson R.E. Lieut Connor also made a trip on one of the Bristol extension biplanes and the *vol plané* by which he landed at the conclusion was especially fine. Capt. Fulton had his biplane out, and made his tests for the RAeC Superior

Certificate, flew to Aldershot and back as mentioned in the last issue. He left Salisbury at 12.10 p.m. and reached Aldershot at 1.20 p.m., while the return journey was commenced at 3 p.m. and completed at 4.10 p.m. Lieut Manisty also made a good flight.

On Thursday and Friday the weather was not very good, and the only work in the air was a number of test flights by Lieut Reynolds with the re-erected biplanes. There was plenty of work, however, going on at the hangars in tuning up the machines, and this was continued on Saturday, when the weather stopped all flying. On Monday, Capt. Fulton was flying in a stiff breeze, but had to come down for adjustments to the engine, after which the machine was in fine form, and was seen flying at a height of 2,000ft, from which it came down with a fine *vol plané,* with the engine stopped. Lieut Hinds was out with the Breguet for a good flight. On Tuesday, work was again confined to the hangars, all the officers finding plenty to do on overhauling their machines.

**Bristol School** – For the purpose of making a height test, on Tuesday of last week, Mr Valentine took up Lieut Williamson on the military monoplane, afterwards performing a fine solo. Tuition work then started in earnest, Pixton taking Lieut Porter, whilst Jullerot carried Lieut MacArthur. The wind was blowing at from 15 to 20 miles per hour all afternoon, making things somewhat difficult.

Prier, with Jullerot as passenger, was on Wednesday up on the military monoplane, making two fine flights during which the machine showed a fine turn of speed. Lieuts. Borton, MacArthur and Porter were taken for their lessons by Busteed, Pixton and Jullerot. These three pupils commenced solo flying almost immediately afterwards, each one showing remarkable promise. At 11.26 a.m., Mt Valentine left for Laffan's Plain, which won him the *brevet superior,* arriving back again at 1.29 p.m. On his return, Mr Valentine and his dog were taken as passengers by Jullerot in a biplane. Prier, with Jullerot as a passenger, did a climbing test on the military monoplane, Valentine, with Mr Thurstan, making a similar test on another machine of the same type. Pixton made his debut as a monoplane flyer, handling the military monoplane with remarkable skill and precision. Two solos by Busteed and Jullerot finished the day.

Valentine, with Lieut Borton as passenger, was up on the military machine on Sunday, circling over Stonehenge for nearly half-an-hour. Jullerot took up Lieut Duff-Dunbar and Lieut Blacklock, and Lieut Bowes, who recently secured his *brevet* on the Bristol, took his fiancé for a passenger flight . . .

# 14

# FORMATION OF THE ROYAL FLYING CORPS

When Blériot completed the first powered flight across the English Channel in July 1909, narrowly beating the English pilot Hubert Latham to the *Daily Mail's* £1000 prize, he confirmed the accuracy of Lord Northcliffe's earlier statement that 'England is no longer an island'.[1] The significance of his comment was the exposure of weaknesses in the country's defences. The British Government had distrusted the Army since the time of Cromwell, and had placed its trust in a strong Royal Navy to protect the British Isles and her interests worldwide. There was some security in the knowledge that the country was surrounded by water, and that Britain's navy was by far the largest in the world. However, Blériot's flight demonstrated that aircraft had the ability to cross easily from one country to another and the seas were no obstacles to their progress. This should have attracted the immediate attention of Whitehall but it was, in fact, another two years before Asquith sent a memorandum to the Committee of Imperial Defence (CID) at the War Office in November 1911 asking them to 'consider the future developments of aerial navigation for both Naval and Military purposes to secure an efficient Air Service'.[2] Although the Air Battalion had been in existence for a few months, it had been poorly resourced and in comparison to their French and German equivalents was little more than a half-hearted experiment. The constitution of the Air Battalion as a unit of the Royal Engineers had provoked much criticism from the outset. The rules governing the hierarchy of its command, whereby the commanding officer was an engineer who need not have any experience as a pilot, was thought to generate a conflict of interest. There were also inconsistencies in individual entitlements. Royal Engineer officers, for example, did not receive an additional pay allowance for 'aeroplane work' as it was considered a normal part of an engineer's career development, whereas officers from other regiments, who were attached to the Air Battalion as Assistant

Engineers, did. For some, the receipt of such allowances negated their right to obtain others, which was seen as a disadvantage. It was hardly fair. Charles Grey, writing of the luddite but otherwise intelligent and academically minded Royal Engineer officers, believed that the Air Battalion was,

> ... being held back by one or two officers of Engineers who should already have retired under the regulation age-limit, are unable to comprehend modern needs, and use all the weight of their position and seniority to prevent the Air Battalion from becoming as it should be... fill it with artillerymen, cavalrymen and guardsmen... infantrymen and even a leaven of engineers, so long as they are caught young, before they become bound up in red tape and theory. Then we shall have the finest corps of air scouts in the world.[3]

On 5 December 1911, Capt. Fulton responded to 'the grievances of the aeroplane officers' and wrote directly to the Under-Secretary of State for War (going above the heads of his immediate superiors). He ventured, 'I have tried to keep it moderate in tone, as I am sure that if I wrote half as strongly as we all feel you would think me guilty of exaggeration.' Fulton continued, 'To achieve efficiency, any future aeroplane corps . . . would have to be entirely extricated from RE control . . . [belonging] to an autonomous aeroplane corps would be a distinction of which anybody would be proud. To be merely attached to the Royal Engineers' Air Battalion, or some such unit, is to get all the kicks and none of the ha'pence.'[4] Fulton's memo was forwarded onto the First Lord of the Admiralty, Winston Churchill, and it arrived on his desk just before he was due to attend a meeting of the Standing Sub-Committee of the CID. Fulton's timing could not have been any better, for on the agenda was Asquith's memorandum. Churchill responded to Fulton, 'Whatever happens the RE must have nothing to do with HM's Corps of Airmen, which should be a new and separate organisation drawing from civilians, as well as military and naval sources . . . [making] military aviation the most honourable, as it is the most dangerous, profession a young man can adopt'.[5]

The Standing Sub-Committee reached the conclusion that the Technical Sub-Committee should create an unaffiliated military or naval aviation service. The Technical Sub-Committee was chaired by Colonel Seely, and comprising Brig. Gen. David Henderson,[6] Col George MacDonogh, Capt. Frederick Sykes and Maj. Donald MacInnes. Among those consulted was Bertram Dickson, who had flown in the Lark Hill Manoeuvres, who said,

> In case of a European war, between two countries, both sides would be equipped with large corps of aeroplanes, each trying to obtain information on the other ... the efforts which each would exert in order to hinder or prevent the enemy from obtaining information ... would lead to the inevitable result of a war in the

Gen. David Henderson sat on the Technical
Sub-Committee. (*Flight*)

air, for the supremacy of the air, by armed
aeroplanes against each other. This fight
for the supremacy of the air in future wars
will be of the greatest importance.'[7]

General David Henderson submitted
the Technical Sub-Committee's
recommendation in February 1912. This
proposed the formation of a flying corps,
comprising five elements: Military and
Naval Wings, a Central Flying School
(CFS), a Reserve and a Royal Aircraft Factory.

On 11 April 1912 the Memorandum on Naval and Military Aviation was
issued and accepted, and two days later, HRH King George V signed a Royal
Warrant establishing the Royal Flying Corps, effective 12 May 1912. Parliament
allocated the sum of £320,000, of which £90,000 was for the construction of
a new airfield on Salisbury Plain (Netheravon), and £32,000 allocated for the
purchase of aeroplanes. The funding announcement was revealed to Parliament
as part of the Army estimates, and it was thought that similar funding would be
offered when the Navy estimates were revealed in due course. This was not to be
the case, however, and the funding had to be split between both services.

David Henderson became the first Commanding Officer of the Royal Flying
Corps (RFC). The military wing of the RFC was formed from the Air Battalion,
and the Royal Balloon Factory Farnborough was renamed as the Royal Aircraft
Factory. Arrangements for recruiting personnel into the reserves were published
in *Flight* in November 1912:

**Outline of Proposals for the Formation of a Special Reserve.**

The following are the draft proposals for the formation of a Special Reserve
of the Military Wing of the Royal Flying Corps. These have not yet been
approved and may be materially amended in detail. The Special Reserve is
mainly required to complete the Airship and Kite Squadron, and the Flying
Depot on mobilisation. The men will, therefore, require to be trained in:

(i.)     The drill of the ground detachments of airships and kites.
(ii.)    The application of their trades in preparing and maintaining aircraft in
the field.

Selected men will, however, be trained in aeroplane work. The period of annual training will probably be the same as that for the Territorial Force, the recruit doing his recruit drills during his first annual training. In addition to the annual training, courses of instruction will be provided for selected non-commissioned officers and men to attend, at which they will be taught the application of their trades to the care and maintenance of aircraft. These courses will extend over one month to six weeks, and will be carried out in Royal Flying workshops at the Central Flying School, or Military Wing.

The men will be recruited chiefly from mechanics of the special trades required, and will enlist for a period of four years, with powers to re-engage under certain conditions. They must accept liability for services abroad in any part of the world, and perform duties in the management of aircraft, whether on land, water, or in the air. For the purposes of administration and training they will be commanded by the Officer Commanding, Military Wing, Royal Flying Corps. The men will receive pay at the Flying Corps rates while performing

Instructors and students of the Air Battalion's first and only training course assembled at Farnborough in April 1912.
*Back Row L to R*: Lieut G.T. Porter, Lieut J.M. Fletcher, Lieut C.M. Waterlow, Lieut B.R.W. Beor, Capt. G.W.P. Dawes, Capt. G.H. Raleigh, Lieut C.A.H. Longcroft, Lieut T.G. Heatherington, Lieut C.T. Carfrae. *Front Row*: Capt. B. Barrington-Kennett, Capt. P.W.L. Broke-Smith, Lieut Col H.R. Cook, Maj. A. Bannerman, Capt. C.R.W. Allen, Capt. A.D. Carden, Capt. E.M. Maitland. (Author's collection)

military duty, and will receive a gratuity of £10 per annum if they carry out their training, and are reported as efficient.[8]

The Naval Wing of the Royal Flying Corps was under the command of the recently promoted Cdr Charles Samson RN, one of the original pilots who Cockburn had trained at Eastchurch in 1911. Samson was very happy to cooperate with his Army colleagues, but his superiors in the Admiralty less so, for whilst it had control of Naval Wing, it was subject to direction on aviation matters from the War Office. By the summer of 1912 an independent Air Department had been created, signalling that the arrogant bureaucrats at the Admiralty were not content to take the inferior position or submit to orders from the 'junior' ministry and wanted direct control of maritime aviation, and in July 1914 the Royal Naval Air Service (RNAS) was established. Differences between the War Office and the Admiralty continued, and would ultimately lead to the decision in 1918 to create the Royal Air Force (See Appendix G).

Just before the RFC was announced, the first military flying training course had assembled. Ten officers who had already obtained their RAeC certificates gathered at Farnborough on 10 April 1912. They had barely begun the first phase of their training, looking at balloons and airships, before the Air Battalion changed to become the RFC. Their training was interrupted, and then resumed at Central Flying School (CFS) later that year. This first CFS course was being assembled in order to address the issue of a shortage of pilots and inadequacies in the training pipeline. The Technical Sub-Committee accepted a proposal, first voiced by the experienced civilian pilot Jimmy Valentine, that the RFC should consider training some of its mechanics as pilots. Not only would the training make them better at their jobs as mechanics, but also they would be available to stand-in to fly the aeroplanes, should the necessity arise. The first two NCOs to earn their RAeC certificates were mechanics from No.3 squadron Lark Hill, who had been taught to fly by Capt. Eustace Loraine. 2nd Cpl. Frank Ridd received his certificate on 4 June 1912 (Royal Aero Club Certificate No.227) and was followed two weeks later by an award to S.Sgt. R. Wilson. Two further certificates were presented to Air Mechanics W. Strugnell and W. McCudden in July and August respectively.

# 15

# CENTRAL FLYING SCHOOL

On 23 April 1912, a Special Army Order authorised the construction of an airfield on former cavalry training gallops to the east of Upavon village, a site that had been chosen by David Henderson. Work began almost immediately to construct eight aeroplane sheds, workshops, accommodation for twenty officers and sixty men, plus a small hospital, costing a total of £25,000. CFS was established at Upavon on 12 May 1912, and the first personnel began to arrive there on 14 June. The commandant was Capt. Godfrey 'Bloody' Paine RN,[1] who had been personally selected by Winston Churchill for the post. Paine had some contact with naval aviation activities as commanding officer of *HMS Actaeon* – a torpedo school ship in Sheerness – and naval personnel at nearby Eastchurch had come under his command, but Paine had never learnt to fly. So Churchill ordered him to get some instruction and gave him just two weeks to qualify. Paine asked Lieut Longmore RN, who had previously served under him onboard *HMS Diamond*, if he could teach him to fly. After just four days intensive tuition Paine received his pilot's certificate on 14 May 1912, but he stayed in London until 25 July to oversee the establishment of CFS from Whitehall. (Paine remained as Commandant CFS until 1917, and became the only British Officer to have served as an Admiral, General and Air Marshall.)

CFS was tasked with providing advanced training to pilots of the Military and Naval Wings of the RFC who already had their Royal Aero Club Certificates. The decision was sound, as the training provided for a RAeC certificate was quite basic. In addition to better practical flying skills, CFS students were taught engine maintenance, meteorology, navigation, aerial photography and signalling. The first CFS instructors were Lieut Col E.H. Cook (Asst Commander), Capt. J. Fulton (who had recently left No.3 Squadron at Lark Hill, passing command to Capt. Brooke-Popham), Capt. E.L. Gerrard RMLI and Lieut A. Longmore RN. The medical officer was Capt. Cordner RAMC. The school used Shorts, Farmans, Avros and Bristols, along with a Deperdussin and Nieuport personally chosen by Gerrard and Longmore and funded by the Admiralty.

Major Hugh Trenchard was appointed as the CFS Adjutant. Trenchard had been given an ultimatum by the War Office. He had returned to England from

Africa in ill health, and his active military service days appeared to be over. He was offered the post of adjutant at CFS if he could learn to fly before his fortieth birthday. Trenchard wasted no time enrolling at Tom Sopwith's Flying School at Brooklands, where Copeland-Perry instructed him. When he passed his final test on 31 July 1912, Sopwith is alleged to have commented, his student would 'Never make a good pilot, but what he lacked in natural ability, he made up for with drive and determination'. Trenchard was awarded his RAeCC on 17 August, the day he started on No.1 Course at CFS along with five other students from the Royal Navy and Royal Marines, ten from the Army and four Special Reserve officers. Coached by Lieut Longmore RN in the school's Maurice Farman, Longmore and Trenchard flew together many times during the course, although in his memoirs Longmore describes the future head of the Royal Air Force as 'Rather big for the passenger seat on my Farman ... perched up on the petrol tank behind the pilot he added considerable resistance and slowed the machine down.'[2] Trenchard would have visited Lark Hill several times before his course ended, but having failed the final written examination he was not among those graduating on 12 December. Nevertheless, he took up his appointment at Upavon, where his responsibilities included the setting and marking of examination papers, whereupon he allegedly 'corrected' his own mistakes and awarded himself a military brevet.

CFS students received a shilling (5p) a day 'flying pay' in addition to their normal rate of pay. On completion of the course they were tested and received either two or four shillings a day, depending upon their flying proficiency. The terms of enlistment published in 1912 states, 'Warrant Officers, NCOs and men in receipt of flying pay will be tested half-yearly, and retention of flying pay by them will depend upon them passing a satisfactory test ... they will be re-classified as 1st or 2nd class flyers in accordance with the standard of proficiency attained by them'.[3]

Completion of the CFS allowed a pilot to become a military flying instructor, and many found themselves teaching other students quite soon after they themselves graduated. Sub-Lieut Chris Draper RNR describes his arrival on No.5 Course in January 1914:

> Upavon consisted entirely of wooden huts. I had a small cabin to myself and shared a military batman with Leo Charlton ... I began in the Avro Flight, commanded by an Army Captain named Maclean, who had obtained his Royal Aero Club Certificate only eight months before me ... Instruction was only given on calm days, over an area called the 'Gallops'. This was a long smooth stretch where we could fly backwards and forwards and make practice landings and takeoffs ... The course came to an end on 26 April 1914. During its 12 weeks, I had got in 19½ hours flying, which was not much better than learning to fly at Hendon. I went home on leave, awaiting the result. It was a nerve-racking time ... In less than a fortnight the Admiralty wrote confirming my appointment to a four-year commission and enclosing a cheque for the £75 it had cost me to learn to fly privately.[4]

# THE STORY BEHIND 'AIRMAN'S CROSS'

Inevitably, there were flying accidents at Lark Hill, but the first unfortunate victim was fifteen-year-old Leonard Williams, the son of a fishmonger from Amesbury. He was standing in a crowd of approximately 300 people, watching the flying on 19 May 1912, when a Bristol Tractor biplane flown by Lieut A.E. Burchardt-Ashton of the 4th Dragoon Guards over ran on landing and ploughed into the crowd. Many were knocked over; some threw themselves flat and allowed the aeroplane to pass over them. It came to a halt and pitched up, turning over onto its back, pinning Williams under the machine. Another lad, Harry Maggs was badly injured, as were two soldiers, Gunner Ratcliffe of the 48th Battery RGA and Gunner Packer of 70th Field Artillery RHA. Williams was removed and an inquest held at Amesbury on 24 May. The solicitor for British & Colonial stated, in the company's defence, it 'had no right to send people off the [flying] ground'. Lieut Burchardt-Ashton was told by the Coroner he was not bound to give evidence, but he still elected to do so. When questioned about the type of aeroplane he was flying, he replied that, with the engine in front of the pilot's seat it 'makes it a little more awkward to see out in the front.' The Coroner turned to questions regarding the crowd, who had gathered in front of the sheds. Burchardt-Ashton said that he had not been able to see them easily, and after landing did not see anyone until there were people all around the aeroplane, and so he was unable to turn. John Huxham was with Williams, and stated there were several aeroplanes flying and that he had not noticed Burchardt-Ashton's aeroplane until it was about 10 yards away and coming towards them. Collyns Pizey gave evidence, and said he felt his staff had done all they could to keep the spectators in a safe area. He confirmed there were no warning signs, only notices saying it was private property. The jury returned a verdict of 'accidental death', and stated that 'They were of the opinion that power should be obtained to exclude the public from the landing approach during the hours of flying, and that danger notice boards to this effect should be erected'.[1] The aeroplane was subsequently dismantled and was never flown again.

Whilst Williams' untimely death is unmarked, two other fatal accidents are commemorated on Salisbury Plain. On Friday, 5 July 1912 Capt. Eustace B. Loraine and Staff-Sergeant Richard 'Bert' Wilson were killed near the junction of the A344, A360 and B3086. They were the first military crew to lose their lives in an aeroplane crash on duty. Loraine was the son of Rear-Admiral Sir Lambton Loraine, and was commissioned into the Grenadier Guards in 1899. He served with distinction in the West Africa Frontier Force under Hugh Trenchard, and was instrumental in his former commanding officer's decision to take up flying. Bert Wilson, on the other hand, had completed an engineering apprenticeship in the Royal Engineers before transferring to the RFC, where his leadership and particular skills with aero-engines earned him promotion and selection as Senior Technician on No.3 Sqn. He had qualified as a pilot himself less than four weeks previously.

They were flying a Nieuport IVG Monoplane on an acceptance flight from Lark Hill, and, when making a tight turn, the aeroplane plunged towards the ground and crashed. From evidence given at their inquest by Capt. Brooke-Popham and Cpl. Ridd it would appear 'Loraine had engendered an excess of confidence in his ability to control the Nieuport machine.'[2] Ridd stated that he had been a passenger in an earlier flight that had taken off at 04.30 a.m., when a similar incident happened. However, as they were flying at a height of around 1,000ft, Loraine was able to recover from the stall and made a safe landing. After some adjustments to the engine, which had been misfiring, Wilson took Ridd's place for a second flight that took off at 05.30 a.m. Loraine flew west towards Shrewton and at the end of Fargo Plain attempted another sharp turn. The aeroplane sideslipped and dived, but as the machine was only at a height of 400ft it hit the ground. Lieut Fox was airborne, and, seeing the crash, landed nearby where he found both men still alive but seriously injured. Wilson had a broken neck and

Lieut Burchardt-Ashton's Bristol Tractor biplane. (J. Fuller)

Newspaper clipping reporting Loraine/
Wilson's accident, 1912. (Unknown)

**TWO ARMY AVIATORS KILLED.**

Machine of British Airmen Turns
Over and Drops 400 Feet.

SALISBURY PLAIN, England, July 5.—
Capt. E. B. Loraine and Sergt. Major
Wilson of the Army Flying Corps were
killed this morning, while flying over the
great military encampment here.
  They were taking their usual early
morning practice, and the aeroplane had
reached a height of 400 feet, when the
machine lost its balance, turned over and
fell with a crash to the roadway.
  Sergt. Major Wilson was killed instantly, but Capt. Loraine lived a short
time, although he was unconscious when
picked up.

Loraine a fractured skull. Fox took off again and went to get assistance, but on his return Wilson was dead. Loraine was transported to Bulford hospital in a horse-drawn ambulance but died ten minutes after admission. The wreckage of the Nieuport was burnt the following morning. Loraine had been due to leave No.3 Squadron at Lark Hill and was going to join CFS as a flying instructor.

A memorial was unveiled by General Smith-Dorrien on 5 July 1913, the first anniversary of the accident, near to the scene of the crash at a junction known locally as 'Airman's Corner'.[3] The inscription on the memorial reads, 'To the memory of Captain Loraine and Staff-Sergeant Wilson who whilst flying on duty, met with a fatal accident near this spot on July 5th 1912. Erected by their comrades'. Unfortunately, records of the inquests following the accident were destroyed in a fire in Salisbury some years later. In 1944 Sir Michael Bruce and several companions were travelling near the area. They claimed to have all seen a small aircraft flying in the vicinity of Airman's Corner and were horrified when it appeared to crash into a wood. They stopped their car and searched the area for survivors but found nothing until they stumbled across the memorial stone. The accident at Airman's Corner, and a number of aeroplane accidents that occurred after the Military Aeroplane Competition at Lark Hill, were to have significant consequences for Military Wing and the whole of the British aeroplane industry (see Chapter 20).

# BRITISH MILITARY AEROPLANE COMPETITION, 1912

As we have already heard, in the autumn of 1911 the French Government held aeroplane trials, witnessed by a large number of politicians, businessmen and key military figures. The Britons attending returned home after the event with a lot to think about. The politician, Mr Sandys, told the house, 'I venture to say considerable fresh light has been thrown upon the value of military aviation by the result of the French manoeuvres on the eastern frontier . . . the general impression conveyed . . . was certainly that the aeroplane is destined in the future to play a very important part in military operations.' He continued, 'I think it is most undesirable that in the event of an emergency we in this country should be dependent upon foreign-built aeroplanes . . . [and] it is highly desirable that some encouragement should be given to British manufacturers of aeroplanes and aircraft generally.'[1] Parliament sought a response, and the Under-Secretary of State for War, Col Seely, said that, 'We are arriving at a point when we think we see our way to choose what is best type, first for teaching people to fly, and secondly, to buy for the purposes of war should war unfortunately break out'[2] adding that there were still many difficulties to overcome. By the end of the year these were resolved and it had been announced that trials similar to those seen in France would be held at Lark Hill. The Military Aeroplane Competition was originally planned to take place in June 1912, but it was delayed until July and then again until Thursday 1 August. This was to be exclusively a War Office event, and although early in 1912 the Admiralty announced their intention to hold a similar competition, the Navy was enjoying a fruitful relationship with both Shorts and Sopwith, and were already developing new designs and procuring suitable aircraft so this event never happened.

Entry to the military competition was open to any aeroplane manufacturer, British or foreign, providing their machine met the entrance criteria, which included: it should be able to take off in a short distance from long grass or

Capt. Godfrey Paine RN and Gen. David Henderson were both judges at the Military Aeroplane Competition. (*Flight*)

harrowed ground and land on rough ploughed land without damage; it must carry a crew of two at a speed of 55mph; be able to attain an altitude of 4,500ft and have a rate of climb of 200ft per min for the first 1,000ft; and be able to maintain a height of 1,500ft for a period of at least one hour. It had to carry enough fuel to fly for 4 hours 30 minutes and be capable of remaining airborne when fully loaded for 3 hours. A panel of judges was appointed, comprising Brigadier General David Henderson (Dir of Military Training), Capt. Godfrey Paine RN (Commandant CFS), Maj. F. Sykes (OC Military Wing RFC) and Mr Mervyn O'Gorman (Superintendant of the Royal Aircraft Factory).

The competitors' machines vied with one another, in tests designed to assess the best performer against the criteria. The winning manufacturers would receive prizes from a total prize fund of £10,000, plus an agreement that the War Office would purchase two of their winning aeroplanes. With a cap on any individual winning more than £5,000, with about one sixth of the top prize being awarded by the French government; the rewards were not massive, however, the promise of becoming the one manufacturer supplying aeroplanes to the British Government was irresistible. The entrants represented both a mixture of radical new ideas and

Deperdussin at Lark Hill, August 1912. (J. Fuller)

tried and tested aeroplanes from larger manufacturers such as Avro, Shorts, Blériot, Bristol and Deperdussin and many smaller constructors whose names have faded with time, such as Mersey and Arial, Borel, Piggott, Hanriot, and Flanders. In all, thirty-two entries were received, although for various reasons a number withdrew and only twenty-five machines arrived on Salisbury Plain for the start. Nine were of foreign manufacture; eight were British machines with foreign engines and only two British through and through (a full list of entrants is contained in Appendix C).

Among the latter was Samuel Cody, who was intending to enter two machines – a monoplane and a very familiar-looking biplane. When Cody left the Balloon Factory he conducted further privately funded trials with British Army Aeroplane No.1. As these experiments progressed, the aeroplane was redesigned and modified, and from time-to-time repaired after minor accidents. It was dismantled early in 1910 and stored at the back of Cody's shed. He built a smaller biplane, No.II, which flew in various events that year. He had earmarked his third aeroplane, the machine used in the Circuit of Britain Air Race, to enter the Military competition alongside his main effort, which was a new design of monoplane. But on 7 December 1911, Lieut Wilfred Parke RN was racing the biplane, with Cody's approval, against fellow officers when he overloaded the aeroplane with fuel and crashed during take-off from Laffen's Plain in a gusty tail-wind. The aeroplane cartwheeled, smashing the fuselage, but Parke walked away uninjured. Cody resurrected his No.II machine, but it had no engine to power it. Remembering the impressive 120hp Austro-Daimler engine fitted to the Etrich monoplane for the Circuit of Britain, Cody recalled its pilot, Lieut H. Bier, an Austrian army officer, had crashed near Hatfield. Enquiries revealed that although the aeroplane had been badly damaged in the accident, the engine was repairable and importantly still in the country.

Cody's monoplane at Laffen's Plain. (Author's Collection)

So Cody made a modest but successful offer, repaired the motor and installed it in the biplane. This machine, with its powerful engine, performed better than he expected. Cody's financial resources were limited, and in order to capitalise on the market of military men who wished to learn to fly, but could not afford the fees, Cody had started providing lessons on the basis that the pupil would pay him when he subsequently received their £75 'refund' upon qualification. A shrewd strategy; however, whilst providing a lesson to Lieut Fletcher in April 1912, Cody asked his student to perform a *vol plané*. He noticed that his student was coming close to a pavilion and fearing they might hit it, Cody leant over and pushed hard on the control column. The biplane dived towards the ground at 75mph and catapulted the two occupants out onto the grass. However, in so doing Cody brushed the engine switch on and the now unmanned aeroplane continued along the ground. It hit a bump and took off for a while before crashing into a tree alongside the canal. Recovering from concussion a few days later Cody inspected the damage, but found it was too extensive. His team had been repairing No.III and so his focus switched back to that machine as far as the biplane entry was concerned.

The accidents with the biplane were a setback; however, Cody had justifiable hopes for his monoplane, as *Flight* commented with the competition approaching: 'it was a very interesting piece of work... for there is none other like it to which it may readily be compared'.[3] It first flew on 21 June; with the Daimler engine fitted to that machine, with its streamlined enclosed cockpit and transparent panels to improve pilot vision, it was an impressive and fast machine. Cody agreed to stage a demonstration of both machines flying together, and whilst Lieut Harvey-Kelly flew the biplane, the monoplane clearly demonstrated its superiority. But on landing, Cody was informed that Harvey-Kelly had hit a tree during his landing and badly damaged that machine. Nine days later, Cody and a team of solicitors appeared at the Treasury Building in Whitehall to have their case against the War Office, for non-payment of £5,000 for the use of his kites and associated patents in 1905,[4] heard by the Chancellor of the Exchequer David Lloyd-George.

Then on 8 July, just three weeks before the competition started, Cody was flying the monoplane at 2,000ft when the engine cut out. He selected an obstacle-free landing area and glided down towards the ground. All seemed well, but just before touchdown the aeroplane pitched and impacted heavily. The propeller disintegrated and the aeroplane broke up. A dazed Cody emerged from the wreckage and noticed the badly mutilated body of a cow lying nearby. Witnesses reported that the animal had been grazing near the landing site, but appeared to be spooked by the shadow of the descending aeroplane. It had charged across Cody's approach path and collided with the aeroplane as it was about to land.

With Cody's best hope disabled he was without a machine, but amazingly still undeterred (possibly because by this stage he was fully committed to aviation and had no other means of income). Mulling over the problem overnight, the following morning Cody telephoned his sons, the team of four mechanics and his seamstresses, rallying them with the confident boast that they could construct another biplane from surviving and stored parts from previous machines and the powerful Daimler engine. The team worked around the clock, improvising and cobbling together a flying machine. On 23 July he heard the result of his legal action, and that he had been awarded £5,000 in compensation, however, this was too late to benefit the latest construction. With the machine complete, Cody decided there was not enough time to dismantle it for transportation to Lark Hill, so he flew it there, arriving with just hours to go before the start of the competition and the entry deadline.

On arrival he would have found the normally laid-back atmosphere that pervaded the Salisbury Plain airfield had changed and Lark Hill had become a hive of activity. Capt. Carden RFC, one of the Capper's team of engineers at the Balloon Factory, was appointed secretary to the committee of judges. It was his responsibility to supervise the mapping out and marking of some 10 square miles of Salisbury Plain that were to be used during the trials, and the erection of temporary storage and accommodation for the teams. A large number of bell tents were erected near to the airfield to accommodate the pilots and mechanics, whilst a marquee nearby served as the mess tent. Harbrows built twelve temporary sheds to house the aeroplanes along Tombs Road, each with an entrant's number painted on the door.[5]

Cody's support team, many of who had cycled the 60 miles from Farnborough, arrived to find that all the accommodation had been taken. The organisers had managed to locate a single room for Cody, but his willing team members were forced to improvise. Such was Cody's determination, and perhaps his sense of fair-play, that he often stayed with his engineers overnight and slept alongside them under the wings of his aeroplane, in the back of their shed or in a large packing crate they borrowed from another entrant.

Of the twenty-five aeroplanes ready to commence the trials, only nineteen machines were considered as serious contenders. *Flight* said Lark Hill, 'Has been

The Bristol Coanda monoplane. (J. Fuller)

the Mecca of the modern aeroplane during the last few weeks, and assembled on its green turf is the best of what the brains of man has thus far devised in the way of flying machines ... It remains for the military authorities to test and try these machines, in order to find out how nearly they satisfy the military point of view [and] for the Government to back the British industry with some very handsome orders.'[6] The Royal Aircraft Factory had sent a BE2, but as a government project it was not allowed to enter the prize competition; it did still attempt each of the trials and was placed at the judges disposal to allow them to move from event to event, providing the pilot and designer Geoffrey De Havilland ample opportunity to demonstrate its capabilities.

The nation's eager anticipation of the event is hard to imagine today. Preparations and developments were reported and closely followed, and the inevitable political furore was echoed in conversations and debate across the country. *Flight* magazine gave the trial extensive coverage, with some editions reporting nothing else. The edition published on 3 August 1912, stated, 'At last the actual event, so long awaited, is upon us and all eyes in the world of flight are directed, metaphorically speaking, towards Salisbury Plain.' *Flight's* editor added, 'Whatever we may have had in mind in criticism of the trials ... [they] have attracted a larger and more representative entry than at one time many believed they would do. As we have so often pointed out in these pages, it is absolutely essential that public opinion should be worked up to the necessary pitch for insisting that our aerial defences should be put on a basis comparable to that of our possible rivals.'

As has already been mentioned, officially, No.3 Squadron had relocated to Upavon for the duration of the trials, whilst BCAC moved their Bristol Flying School operation to Brooklands, but the staff remained on site to help support the BCAC entrants; the military fliers were not going to miss this opportunity to see what was going on and were frequent visitors back at Lark Hill, as were the members of staff at CFS Upavon. To encourage public support, *Flight* magazine

Personnel of No.3 Squadron Royal Flying Corps were regular visitors to the competition. (Unknown)

Cody with Army personnel at Lark Hill.
(J. Fuller)

published a sketch map, and suggested vantage points where spectators may safely observe the trials, offering the advice, 'There will be no tests on August Bank Holiday nor on any Sunday, that is to say, no flying under official conditions, but machines may be expected out on any fine day'.[7] Contemporary photographs show the event did indeed draw in spectators; however, comment on favourable weather proved to be optimistic, readers who are familiar with the weather on Salisbury Plain will realise it is unpredictable at the best of times, and a regime of bad weather and strong winds settled over the area for most of August. It had been the intention to fly a blue flag over the sheds at Lark Hill when the weather was fit for flying, but unfortunately the flag was not flown as often as the organisers might have hoped and the first ten days produced only thirty-eight suitable flying hours. *Flight* was later to comment, 'In the memory of man, I imagine there has never been such an August anywhere, and that it should have occurred on an official aviation meeting, of all events, is nothing short of the height of irony'.[8] Jack T.C. Long, writing the history of No.3 Squadron, says 'About two hundred members of parliament came down to Salisbury Plain on the 8th August to witness the competition of the aeroplanes in the military trials. The wind was judged to be too tempestuous for flying and the flights were limited to a few short circuits round the airfield in the afternoon'.[9] With winds gusting over 45mph at one point, the roof lifted completely off one of the sheds used by Coventry Ordnance. When asked if he would demonstrate his aeroplane, Cody replied, 'I only have one aeroplane entered . . . why should I risk it in this weather, especially as it is already doing so well in the trials?'[10]

Perhaps an example of opportunism, the judges reacted to the inclement weather conditions and introduced a new test that was not in the original programme – the Rough Weather test. It is worth noting the conditions proved that the machines themselves were capable of flight in stronger winds than was thought possible, but the physical toll on the pilot flying in these conditions was something they had not expected, 'For a quarter of an hour, Pixton fought the gust, which ranged from 17mph to 47mph in velocity . . . just after landing the wind–gauge registered 50mph, so there was no question of the conditions quieting down when the machine had once got into the air . . . The machines behaved splendidly, and it must have been in excellent trim, for the gust jerked the control out of Pixton's hands on many occasions.'[11]

Whenever flying was impossible the teams busied themselves preparing or repairing their machines and, when the essential work was done, found their own entertainment. Cody annoyed competitors by lassoing members of the other teams as they passed his shed, and was the main instigator of a number of competitive games. Unexpectedly, he appears to have developed a taste for the very English game of cricket.

The tests began, but things did not always go as well as they might. The first challenge was the speed test, in which the teams had to dismantle the aircraft so it could be transported on a cart and then, against the clock, assemble their machine and prepare it for flight. Charlie Tye, one of the Handley Page engineers, recalls, 'On the first day of the test, packing cases, like a row of immense match boxes, stretched out across the plain. On a signal from the judges each team had to break open their container and assemble the aeroplane. The time taken varied considerably. A.V. Roe's machine was completed and ready to fly in a commendably short time of fourteen and a half minutes. On the other hand, five men laboured for nearly nine and a half hours to get their Maurice Farman into flying shape.'[12]

The Avro Type G was a biplane with an enclosed cockpit; protection for its crew that would have certainly attracted favourable comment had it not severely reduced the pilot's forward visibility. The company had intended to send two machines to Lark Hill, but the Green engine for the second airframe was not ready in time. The pilot of the sole machine was Lieut Wilfred Parke RN, the same pilot who had played a disastrous role in Cody's preparations. He damaged the Type G in a crash on 7 August that necessitated the machine be returned to the factory. Just twelve days later, the Avro G was back at Lark Hill, and the speed of its

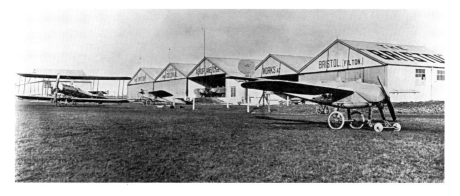

Bristol aeroplanes outside the sheds during the competition. (Bristol Airchive)

reappearance suggests the company simply removed the ABC engine and refitted it in the other airframe, which was then rebadged, and returned, as entrant No.7.

On 12 August, whilst the competitors were proving their ability to fly at 4,500ft, Geoffrey de Havilland decided to attempt a new British altitude record. With Maj. Sykes as a passenger, de Havilland took off in the BE2, and climbing faster than any of the other competitors reached an altitude of 10,560ft and so claimed the record. But in the process, de Havilland had flown above layers of cloud and got lost to the northeast of Salisbury Plain. After trying to determine his whereabouts he descended to low-level near Newbury, where he read the nameplates on the railway station at Hermitage, and from there followed the railway line back to Amesbury.

The following day Robert Fenwick was less fortunate. He took off alone at 6.15 p.m. for a practice flight in the Mersey monoplane. It was only his third ascent in the competition. Spectators watching the take-off noted the aeroplane appeared unstable. The wind was quite gusty, as reported by Harry Busteed who was also airborne at that time, so this was not unusual, and it was thought the pilot would steady the machine in due course. However, at a height of about 300ft, whilst still in sight of the sheds, the Mersey was seen to fall and crash. The following poignant letter was published by *Flight* shortly after the accident.

As the late R.C. Fenwick's partner, and an eyewitness of the terrible disaster which cost him his life, I would like to give as clear an account as I can of the accident, the accounts which have appeared in the papers being, as usual, very far from correct. Fenwick began his last flight shortly after 6 p.m., in a dead calm. The machine got off quickly and climbed steadily and straight to about 300ft. At this height he seemed to encounter a strong wind but in no case can it be said that the wearing of a helmet has occasioned a fatality. While I am not of opinion that any definite rule should be laid down as to the wearing of a safety helmet, yet I hope that all flying schools, especially monoplane schools, will gusts. I could see that he was warping, and a moment afterwards he dived to gain speed. After a short dive, seeming to find that all was calm again, he again began to climb, but again encountered gusts and dived. It seemed that the second dive was meant to be continued till the machine reached the ground, as it was continued for 50 or 100ft perfectly evenly and steadily. Instead of continuing, however, the dive changed to a vertical drop, the machine falling until it was out of sight. The machine seemed perfectly under control until the end, and was not in any way 'blown over' or overpowered by the gusts – as some papers have stated.

The really inexplicable part is why a seemingly well-controlled *vol plané* should have changed into a vertical drop. The machine may have dived into a bad pocket and not have had time to recover. Or poor Fenwick's feet may have slipped forward off the rudder bar, throwing him against the elevator, and so causing the drop. He was wearing smooth-soled rubber shoes and had been walking on wet grass, which may have caused the slip. We shall never know. All controls were in order. The wind gauge during the time of his flight showed a dead calm, an absolutely sudden gust of some 20mph, followed by a few seconds' calm, and then another violent gust, followed by a wind rising till late at night.

Several officers who were standing with me watching the machine can corroborate my account. Fenwick was not only my partner, but a very intimate and dear friend, and his sudden and tragic death was a terrible shock. In justice to a sound designer, skilful mechanic, and careful pilot, and in justice to a good machine, I cannot let the ordinary newspaper reports go unchallenged, but am sending you an account of what I personally saw. May I take this opportunity of thanking all those, too numerous to thank individually, who have shown their kindness and sympathy during the last few days.

S. T. Swaby, South Shields[13]

The machine was completely wrecked and Fenwick was killed instantly. Later that morning, the wreckage of the Mersey was burnt. The RAeC enquiry would judge that the accident was caused by inadequacies in the monoplane design; it also recommended that in future all crash wreckage should be retained to help such enquiries, in the hope that it would prevent recurrences and further unnecessary loss of life. Sydney Sippe had a luckier escape than Fenwick whilst flying a Hanriot on the morning of Thursday August 22. His monoplane pitched onto its nose, landing on a ploughed field, to prove the machine's rough-ground landing and take-off ability. Fortunately, it did little damage and Sippe was uninjured and able to continue with the trials. (This particular test being won by a French Deperdussin No.26 flown by Maurice Prevost, who got airborne in just 132 yds (120m).) One of the best performers in the short landing trial was Cody, because he employed the simple expedient of fitting a rudimentary braking system to his aeroplane. Meanwhile, other competitors were hoping to complete their three-hour endurance flights. Frederick Raynham was one of the

Advertisement for Green Aero Engines. (*Flight*)

first airborne in the Coventry Ordnance machine designed by Howard Wright and W.O. Manning. The two designers were no strangers to Salisbury Plain, having been Horatio Barber's partners at ASL here in 1909. *Flight's* technical editor felt that their promising machine had not lived up to expectations, and lamented the lack of pilots such as Gordon England, who had the skill and knowledge to advise their engineers how to get the best from the engines. However, even such technical proficiency could not avoid some incidents. BCAC had entered two of England's GE2 biplanes into the competition. The Daimler-Mercedes engine fitted to Pixton's machine (entrant No.13) could not be made to run properly, and it quickly became apparent neither was as competitive as the company's Coanda monoplanes, and both GEs were withdrawn.

However, England decided to continue to fly for his own entertainment. One morning he took off in a machine that had just emerged from repairs in the shed. During the maintenance the mechanic, Temple Robins, had lashed together the tail control wires and these were still tied together. The machine was so well balanced that England flew for an hour and a half without realising he had no elevator control. The lack of control was only apparent when he tried to flatten out on landing. However, being an experienced pilot he managed to control the landing by use of the throttle, as Dallas Brett described it, 'The pilot pulled the nose up by opening the throttle for a moment and thus arranged the impact without breaking anything.'[14] Readers might think England neglectful for not conducting pre-flight checks, which is considered an essential procedure today, however, it was not thought to be as important then. England's general regard for his own safety might, however, be questioned when the reader learns that earlier in his career he willingly assisted José Weiss to conduct glider experiments. This involved him being 'shot forwards over a precipice'.[15] With only rudder controls he could do 'Little to influence events subsequent to the launch, his but to reason why and make notes of the machine's behaviour . . . until such time as the apparatus returned to earth of its own volition.'[16] Brett calls him very brave, but I suspect others will agree with the author that this is not the particular quality they might attribute to such behaviour.

The Bristol GE2, designed by Gordon England, was not a success. (J. Fuller)

# 18

# THE PARKE DIVE

On Sunday 25 August, having been hampered by bad weather earlier in the week, the Avro team sought permission to complete their endurance flight (the planners had originally decreed that Sundays would be a day of rest and there would be no flying on the Sabbath). The judges conceded, and when Lieut Wilfred Parke RN and his observer, Lieut Le Breton RFC, took off at 06.04 a.m. in the Avro Type G biplane (entrant No.7), neither of the crew could have known they were about to experience 'one of the worst experiences from which any pilot has extracted his machine in absolute safety'.[1] At 09.10 a.m., the test completed, Parke started his recovery back to Lark Hill from overhead Upavon. It was a bright morning with some cloud and a southerly wind blowing 10–15kts. Arriving over the flying ground at a height of 700ft, Parke decided to enter a spiral glide to land in front of the aeroplane sheds – a standard manoeuvre that was not as ostentatious as it might perhaps sound. He closed the throttle and turned left downwind. Halfway around the turn, Parke says he was descending too steeply and did not have enough to bank on, and whilst correcting this, the aircraft entered a spiral nose-dive. He opened the throttle, hoping the propeller might pull the nose up, but to no effect, and spectators having breakfast below watched horror stricken, waiting for the seemingly inevitable end. Parke pulled back on the elevator and applied full left rudder, but was still spinning. Thrown against the side of the cockpit he took his hand off the controls, to steady himself against a strut, and reversed the rudder to hard-over right. Instantly, and without any jerkiness, the aeroplane pulled out of the spin at just 50ft above the ground, and flew-off in a level attitude. Parke took control and positioned the aeroplane to make an into-wind landing without further incident. The only damage was some slight stretching to wires under the main wing. Parke was not the first pilot to have recovered from a spin (Freddie Raynham had done so in 1911, but was unable to recall his actions). The recovery was much talked about and became known as 'Parke's Technique', or 'The Parke Dive'. Incredibly, the manoeuvre was not taught to pilots under training until after the start of the First World War, but is still used today as the standard spin recovery. Parke was killed three months later whilst flying from Hendon to Oxford in a Handley Page Type F that suffered a loss of engine power and crashed onto Wembley golf course on 11 December 1912.

# 19

# AND THE WINNER IS …

Many years later, the historian J.M. Bruce wrote an article on the Lark Hill competition for *Aeroplane Monthly*, entitled 'A Pointless Exercise', and indeed at the end of the trials the final result would seem to suggest they failed to achieve their goal. There was but one British aeroplane in the top five, the remainder of the machines were predictably of French design. Contemporary opinion judged the best performing aeroplane to be the Hanriot Monoplanes, but the judges awarded the prize to Cody's Cathedral biplane. This was undoubtedly a political decision, for whilst Parke described it as a delightful machine to pilot, in truth it had failed to complete one of the tests, and was out performed in many others. It was unsuited to mass production and offered no protection to its crew. Cody received £5,000 and a message of congratulations from HRH King George V, who continued his habit of addressing him as 'Colonel' Cody (it appears even the monarch was able to confuse Samuel and William Cody). Responding to this mistake, with amusement, Cody said 'The King can do no wrong … as His Majesty has referred to me as Colonel Cody, so in future Colonel Cody it has to be.'[1] Cody appeared to enjoy his new 'honorary' rank, but the members of the Royal Aero Club who awarded him their highest award, a Gold Medal, for his successes, preferred the nickname 'Daddy' Cody.

Cody's biplane outside the MAC Sheds, August 1912. (Author's Collection)

The ultimate goal, he might have hoped for, of supplying aeroplanes to the military, eluded him. The War Office bought two aeroplanes to comply with their obligation to the competition winner, but the mass-procurement decision went in favour of the Royal Aircraft Factory BE2, with production being contracted out to the established British manufacturers. What happened to the two Cody V biplanes? Both were based at Farnborough until April 1913. Lieut L.C. Rodgers-Harrison was flying No.301 over the airfield, when, descending from 1,200ft, the aeroplane entered a steep dive and suddenly disintegrated in mid-air, with pieces of the aeroplane falling to the ground into adjacent fields. Rogers-Harrison was killed. It was suggested the parts used to assemble the aeroplane were worn out. Four months later, Cody himself was killed when a seaplane that he was preparing to enter yet another competition, crashed on 7 August. On his death, the RFC gave Cody's second biplane to the Science Museum, where it remains on display to this day beside Amy Johnson's Gypsy Moth, and Alcock and Brown's Vickers Vimy.

# MONOPLANES GROUNDED

Following the Airman's Cross crash, and Fenwick's accident during the military trails, a number of other accidents happened in quick succession. The RFC lost Capt. P. Hamilton and Lieut Wyness-Stuart on 6 September 1912, when their Deperdussin crashed near Hitchin; and four days later, Edward Hotchkiss, Bristol's Chief Instructor, and Lieut Bettington were killed whilst flying Coanda Monoplane No.263 from Lark Hill to Cambridge. Their aeroplane was seen near Oxford, diving steeply towards the ground, when at a height of about 200ft the fabric tore off the right-hand wing and the machine crashed into the ground, killing both occupants instantly. Hotchkiss was one of the Bristol Flying School instructors, but on this occasion was flying as an officer in the RFC Reserve and became the first in that force to die on duty. The RAeC inquiry established beyond reasonable doubt that the 'quick-release' catch, fitted as a requirement of the military trial, came open in flight and a piece of metal had broken from the fuselage and torn through the wing.

Deperdussin with one of the several types affected by the decision to ground Army monoplanes. (J. Fuller)

On 14 September, the Under Secretary for War grounded all Military Wing's monoplanes, an announcement that had a massive impact on British aeroplane manufacturers.[1] The Blériot Company had weathered similar restrictions when the French Government reacted to a number of similar crashes in 1911, and had previously strengthened the wing bracing wires on their machines. Post-First World War analysis revealed the real cause of wing failures was actually the wing loading; however, by fitting stronger wires Blériot had reduced the possibility that excessive loading would cause a failure.

A committee, comprising Brig. Gen. Henderson, Maj. Sykes, Maj. Brooke-Popham and Lieut Spencer RN, was convened to search for inherent flaws in monoplane design. Henderson submitted the committee's report in February 1913 and, after all RFC monoplanes had been modified at the Royal Aircraft Factory and any quick-release catches removed, they were allowed to fly again that spring. However, monoplane development had been set back several years.

Throughout this affair, Gordon England had been expressing his concerns, in particular over the structural integrity of the Coanda monoplanes, and begged his directors to suspend its use. He was unaware that his brother Geoffrey had recently joined BCAC and was now involved in test-flying the machines. When Gordon learnt of this he asked another manufacturer to offer Geoffrey a better paid position; however, BCAC simply increased Geoffrey's wages and retained his services. Gordon resigned in protest. Sadly, his concerns were well founded, and one month later Geoffrey was killed when the wings came off the Coanda monoplane he was test-flying, prior to delivery to Rumania, and he crashed onto Salisbury Plain in March 1913.

# BUSINESS AS NORMAL

It appears that little thought was given during the trials to preserving the Sun Gap, but the issue seems to have arisen the following year. Although after the trials most of the temporary sheds were dismantled and removed to Farnborough, it appears that some that remained at Lark Hill were blocking the gap. On 4 March 1913, the Commanding Officer No.3 Sqn wrote to Lieut Col Wright RE, the Chief Royal Engineer at Salisbury Plain. Wright responded promptly, stating, 'I do not think there is any undertaking on the part of the W.O. to maintain this gap . . . I do not consider I should be justified in recommending expenditure of W.O. funds on removing a shed to avoid the possibility of interfering with the sun's rays falling on Stonehenge.'[1] Brooke-Popham forwarded the response onto the RFC headquarters at Farnborough, and with the solstice approaching, Maj. Sykes, the Officer Commanding Military Wing, contacted the Director of Fortification and Works on 17 May 1913, and stated, 'The question of the Sun Gap will occur almost immediately now, and I would request that the two remaining Harbrow temporary sheds should be taken down and stored. I can now arrange as regards housing of machines without them.'[2] Whether this removal then happened is uncertain. When Salisbury Plain was hit by hurricane force winds in March 1914, *Flight* magazine reported, 'Hurricane over 80 miles an hour last week. All the second line of Army sheds were uprooted by the wind and flew into bits, totally demolished. Parts of the roofs were found half a mile away.'[3] It is not clear from the report which sheds were destroyed, but it is a clear reference to the fact some of the trial sheds had remained on site sometime after the event.

The Bristol Flying School returned from Brooklands, and No.3 Squadron from Upavon, whereupon they resumed their training and experimental work. Perhaps driven by the still lamentable facilities at Lark Hill and the bitter cold, the squadron officers continued to use The Bustard Inn as their Officers' Mess, whilst the other ranks were moved to Bulford Camp and then into Netheravon Cavalry Barracks.

On 16 April 1913, Lieut Cholmondley of No.3 Squadron departed from Lark Hill for Upavon one evening, in a Maurice Farman, and made what is recorded as the first night landing in Britain.[4] The flight, made by the light of a full moon, was uneventful, however, Cholmondley experienced some difficulty on final approach when he found the moonlight was less illuminating below 100ft above ground level. Cholmondley went onto to perform other night flights, landing by the light of an open hanger door. After his colleague Lieut Carmicheal suggested fitting small lights to the compass and tachometer, and paraffin 'gooseneck' flares were used to mark out the landing area, night flying became a regular practice for the RFC.

On 30 August 1913, the *Salisbury Journal* published an article under the heading 'Live Shell & Ball Cartridge – Realistic Exercises on Salisbury Plain – Scouting by Aeroplane'. It reported:

> A very interesting feature was the use of aeroplanes to direct the fire of artillery against a concealed battery ... There were three or four aeroplanes belonging to the Military Wing of the Royal Flying Corps at the exercise, and though there was a fresh wind, they were continually at work and sent down constant and good reports of the positions of the dummies. These reports were thrown down in little bags with streamers attached and orders were sent up to the flying men by cipher in the form of block letters of white canvas, pegged out or laid flat on the ground. These letters, it was found, had to be 6 feet long to be read with ease ...

The report concludes, 'The modest success was striking enough to make it clear that nothing should be spared to continue these experiments and to fit out each brigade of artillery with a supply of planes and fliers.' Holt-Thomas, one of the journalists who witnessed Dickson's flights in 1910, who had also been observing recent manoeuvres, commented, 'I can only say I was astounded ... I refer to the superb skill and excellent organisation of the aerial forces, which though small now only wants increasing in numbers and size.' He must have been pleased to learn from the spring of 1914 onwards that the War Office intended to increase the RFC's aviation budget to £1 million, and that the Admiralty was being similarly generous with the newly formed Royal Naval Air Service.

Meanwhile, BCAC had also been busy. The Filton factory had rebuilt one of the Bristol Coanda monoplanes (No.121) as the prototype TB8 (Tractor biplane) hydroplane No.15, and it was brought to Lark Hill for test-flying before being delivered to the Naval Wing. The conversion from monoplane was probably initiated as a reaction to the monoplane ban, however, as the reader will have already noted, such radical redesign of aircraft was not uncommon at this time. The Bristol Flying School had resumed training too, and Pizey had a close escape on 26 May whilst flying with H. Fellowes near Salisbury. Their Coanda BR7 biplane was over the outskirts of the city at a height of about 1,200ft, when suddenly the carburettor caught fire. Pizey immediately turned off the fuel and commenced a steep *vol plané*, but the rush of air as they descended only seemed to fan the flames that licked around the passenger seat. Fellowes was sent to stand up and cling to the aeroplane struts. Pizey, however, remained in his seat, clinging to the controls, and despite burnt hands made a successful forced landing. The two men jumped from the aircraft just before the fuel tank exploded.

Less fortunately the school lost one of their students on 17 July 1913. Alexander Hewetson was a forty-four-year-old major in the Royal Artillery, and married to Madame Mathilde Franck, the first female professional pilot. He had been under instruction at Lark Hill for two months, when he took off from Lark Hill at 6.20 p.m. in a Bristol Dickson-Prier 'Sociable' monoplane, to take his RAeC Flying Test. He was flying the required 'figures-of-eight' when he over-banked and stalled at about 100ft above the ground. After the accident his Instructor, Henri Jullerot, said he considered it inadvisable 'that men of the major's age should take up flying.'[5] Hewetson's death is the second fatality recorded on site that is still memorialised today; a stone cross was erected by the side of the A344, west of Stonehenge, some way from the scene of the accident. A less conspicuous memorial plaque, within a small fenced enclosure, may be found today at the site of the crash on the old flying ground (Grid Reference SU1395439).

Maj. Hewetson's crash site, with the flying sheds in the background. (Author's Collection)

Another unfortunate accident befell the flying school on 26 January 1914. Mr Warren Merriam, an instructor at Bristol Flying School at Brooklands, was helping out at Lark Hill. Despite being particularly shortsighted, Merriam was regarded as a great pilot and a very popular instructor. That morning he took off in a Bristol Coanda that had been modified with side-by-side seating, with his pupil Mr G.L. Gipps. The aircraft was not fitted with an air speed indicator, rev counter or bank indicator, and neither pilot was strapped in, nor wore any head protection. After completing one circuit, the aeroplane stalled and dived into the ground. Merriam suffered serious injury and Gipps was killed. The accident enquiry pronounced the cause as pilot error, in that Merriam had been unable to respond to an incorrect input by Gipps. Around this time, but as far as may be ascertained with no link to the accidents, Henri Coanda stopped work on a new monoplane project and left BCAC. His place as chief designer was taken by Frank Barnwell, who adapted Coanda's design for the Italian government known as the SB5 into a single-seat biplane No.206 flew at Lark Hill in February 1914, and was exhibited at Olympia on 16 March under the name Bristol Baby, where it was 'the smallest biplane... but without doubt the most sensational.'[6] When Charles Grey had seen Harry Busteed testing the biplane at Lark Hill Gray was very impressed and described it in his column in *The Aero* as 'the fastest aeroplane in England today'. After Olympia, the biplane was taken to Filton for some modifications, and by the time it had returned it had acquired a new name, the Bristol Scout. In a number of variants, over 360 Scouts were built and flew with both the RFC and RNAS during the First World War.

# THE MOVE TO NETHERAVON

After the formation of the RFC in 1912, the War Office had commissioned the building of an airfield to the north east of Lark Hill, near Mile Ball on the eastern side of the Avon valley. The site lay along the boundary between the villages of Fittleton and Figheldean, with buildings in both parishes; however, while construction work was in progress, service personnel were housed in the former cavalry school at Netheravon, and it is perhaps for that reason the airfield acquired that name when it opened in June 1913. Offering better accommodation than Lark Hill, No. 3 Squadron RFC seized the opportunity to relocate as soon as the new airfield was opened, and for a short period in 1914, Netheravon was used by CFS, but for most of the First World War it would be an operational base.

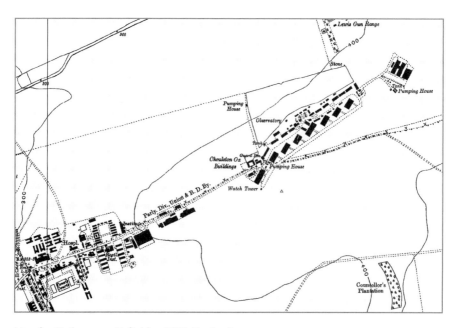

Map for Netheravon Airfield, c.1922. (Author)

Biplanes at
Netheravon for the
Concentration Camp.
(*Flight*)

In June 1914 the whole of the Military Wing was gathered together at Netheravon in a so-called 'Concentration Camp' [1] to explore and practice the mobilisation of the entire corps. The aim of Maj. Frederick H. Sykes, Commanding Officer of Military Wing and organiser of the camp, was to gather together his squadrons and units en-masse for a month of solid training, day and night, under conditions as similar as possible to those they might expect on active service. Seventy flying machines, over 100 flying officers, 150 transport vehicles and 650 air mechanics assembled at the new airfield.

Numbers 2, 3, 4 and 5 Squadrons were presently equipped with BEs, Farmans and Avros, with a few Sopwiths and some Blériot monoplanes. Of note is that No.1 Squadron (formerly No.1 'The Gas Company') had handed over all balloons and airships to Naval Wing and was in the process of equipping as an aeroplane squadron, along with Nos 6 and 7 Squadrons. It was undoubtedly an impressive demonstration of force and represented the largest concentration of aerial strength seen in any army to date. However, *Flight* pondered at the time, 'What France or Germany could do under similar circumstances we frankly do not know, further than they could make a much better numerical showing.'[2]  On Monday 22 June, the assembled aircraft took part in the King's Birthday Parade Review on Salisbury Plain, and later in the week, the Prime Minister, who was accompanied by Mr Harold Baker MP and Gen. Hubert Hamilton, visited the camp. The party drove from Andover to one of the temporary landing grounds, before moving onto Netheravon itself. After lunch they saw several flying demonstration, inspected No.2 Squadron and visited the Sergeants' Mess and a number of barrack blocks, before moving on to inspect CFS at Upavon. At the end of the camp, the Commanding Officer RFC received the following letter from the War Office, 'I am to inform you that the Secretary of State for War has expressed his appreciation of the excellent arrangements made for the Concentration of the Military Wing of the Royal Flying Corps at Netheravon, and the good work that has been carried out by the Corps this last month.'[3] Within a couple of months Britain was at war.

# 23

# FOR VALOUR

Many of the aviators flying at Lark Hill subsequently received awards for their gallantry during the war. Two men were to receive the ultimate award, the Victoria Cross. The first was Lionel W. Brabazon-Rees, who was commissioned in the Royal Garrison Artillery and learnt to fly at Lark Hill at the end of 1912, receiving Royal Aero Club Certificate No.392 on 7 January 1913. After serving in the West African Frontier Force, he transferred to the Royal Flying Corps in August 1914, becoming an instructor at Upavon. Flying the Vickers FB.5 in 1915, he saw action with 11 Sqn, for which he received the Military Cross before assuming command of 32 Sqn in January 1916.

On 1 July 1916, Maj. Brabazon-Rees was patrolling in an Airco DH.2 when he sighted what he thought to be a bombing party of British machines returning home.

He went up to escort them, but on getting nearer discovered they were a party of enemy machines, about ten in all.

Major Rees was immediately attacked by one of the machines, and after a short encounter it disappeared behind the enemy lines, damaged. Five others then attacked him at long range, but these he dispersed on coming to close quarters, after seriously damaging two of the machines. Seeing two others going westwards, he gave chase to them, but on coming nearer he was wounded in the thigh, causing him to lose temporary control of his machine. He soon righted it, and immediately closed with the enemy, firing at a close-contact range of only a few yards, until all his ammunition was used up. Rees turned away as the enemy machine retreated and landed back behind British lines.

The second VC recipient was James 'Jimmy' McCudden. Having joined the Royal Engineers as a bugler at the age of fifteen, McCudden applied for transfer to the RFC as a mechanic. He was posted to No.3 Sqn on 15 June 1913 (the day before the squadron moved over to Netheravon). His first day of duty was inauspicious. He had been ordered to familiarise himself with the aeroplane's engines and told to practice propeller-swinging on a Caudron parked in a corner of the hangar. After lunch he was given the task of rubbing rust off the rigging wires of a Maurice Farman. Tiring of this rather monotonous job, he went back to the Caudron. However, someone had been working on the machine and left it switched on. When he swung the prop the engine burst into life and the aeroplane leapt forwards. Jimmy threw himself to the ground and avoided being decapitated by the narrowest of margins. The Caudron rolled across the hangar and collided with the Farman, slicing off part of its wing and damaging the tail boom. McCudden ran over and switched off the Caudron's engine. He was placed under arrest by the squadron sergeant major, and duly appeared before Capt. Maitland. Handing out his punishment, Maitland said, 'Not a good start is it,'[1] but then praised Jimmy's quick thinking. During the First World War he went to France and was awarded the Military Medal and Croix de Guerre, before returning to England for pilot training in 1916, and served with Nos. 20 and 29 Squadron before being commissioned in January 1917.

By April 1918 McCudden had claimed fifty-four victories, including several encounters with members of Von Richtofen's 'Flying Circus'. He was awarded the Victoria Cross, and with typical modesty he did not even inform his family about the award.

For most conspicuous bravery, exceptional perseverance, and a very high devotion to duty. Captain McCudden has at the present time accounted for 54 enemy aeroplanes. Of these, 42 have been destroyed, 19 of them on our side of the lines. Only 12 out of the 54 have been driven down out of control. On two occasions, he had totally destroyed 4 two-seater enemy aeroplanes on the same day, and on the last occasion all 4 machines were destroyed in the space of one hour and thirty minutes. While in his present squadron, he has participated in 78 offensive patrols, and in nearly every case has been the leader. On at least 30 occasions, whilst with the same squadron, he has crossed the lines alone, either in pursuit or in quest of enemy aeroplanes. The following incidents are examples of the work he has done recently: on 23 December 1917, when leading his patrol, 8 enemy aeroplanes were attacked between 1430 and 1550 and of these 2 were shot down by Captain McCudden in our lines; on the morning of the same day, he left the ground at 1050 and encountered 4 enemy aeroplanes and of these he shot 2 down; on 30 January 1918, he, single-handed, attacked 5 enemy scouts, as a result of which 2 were destroyed. On this occasion, he only returned home when the enemy scouts had been driven far east; his Lewis gun ammunition was all finished and the belt of his Vickers gun had broken. As a patrol leader he has at all times shown the utmost gallantry and skill, not only in the manner in which he has attacked and destroyed the enemy, but in the way he has, during several aerial fights, protected the newer members of his flight, thus keeping down their casualties to a minimum. This officer is considered, by the record he has made, by his fearlessness, and by the great service which he has rendered to his country, deserving of the very highest honour.[2]

McCudden, who was one of the most decorated combatants during the First World War, died when the engine on his SE5's engine cut out shortly after take off in July 1918. He had been trained, like all pilots, not to attempt to turn back to the airfield, but he attempted to do just that and crashed.

# 24

# THE LARK HILL MILITARY LIGHT RAILWAY (LMLR)

Today, it is perhaps difficult to imagine what Salisbury Plain looked like at the time, when all but the main roads were narrow tracks, dust-bound in summer and a sea of mud in the winter. Troops training in the area would have been expected to travel by train to the nearest railway station at Porton and then march 8 miles to new camps that were being built at Durrington or Lark Hill. Several proposals for railway lines, including one connecting the main line at Salisbury to that at Pewsey, via Durrington, Netheravon and Upavon, and another from Grateley, past Stonehenge to Shrewton, and Tilshead to Lavington, were vetoed, and the initial line running alongside what is now the northern boundary of Boscombe Down airfield as far as Amesbury was opened in 1902. As the army build-up continued, that line was extended north to Bulford Camp in 1906, and the line, which was to become the LMLR, was proposed at an estimated cost of some £62,500. Sir John Jackson, whose company had previously worked on the construction of Tower Bridge and the Manchester Ship Canal, and had been given the task of building the hutted camps that were appearing around Lark Hill, set about building the railway line to transport building materials to the site.

The line branched from the Amesbury–Bulford line 700 yards north of the Ratfyn 'Wheelbarrow' junction, where a signal box was used between 1914 and 1919, and crossed the River Avon via substantial girder bridge and through an un-gated level crossing over the Upavon road, known as Countess Crossing. The reversing triangle at Strangeways, midway between the level crossing at Countess and Lark Hill, has caused historians some confusion. In his book on the military railways, Grayer suggests, 'It only became a turning facility after its original purpose was superseded',[1] namely as a junction for a further line which would loop around and rejoin the main track before it crossed The Packway. The main line continued to a small station at Strangeways, where remains of the platform can be found in the undergrowth today. Past this, the line split and a

Lark Hill Military Light Railway, River Avon crossing. (J. Fuller)

section known as the Flying Shed siding divided the now inactive flying ground, whilst the main section of track weaved across the western edge of the airfield towards Rollestone Camp. The main line turned south to Fargo Hospital, where two further branches served the Handley Page hangars and Stonehenge Airfield, then continued south to Lake Down Airfield. In 1914 the Lark Hill Military Light Railway (LMLR) was completed. Running a total distance of more than 10 miles, including all the sidings and spurs, it was the longest railway running across Salisbury Plain.

Operated by Southern Command of the Military Camp Railways, a small company of Royal Engineers was housed in a small camp at Countess Crossing. The LMLR was primarily intended for the movement of stores and ammunition, and was never used for routine passenger transport, although undoubtedly some 'troop trains' were run and special trains were laid on at weekends. Two locomotive sheds and a water tower were erected at Ratfyn to store a number of locomotives that were known to have operated on the line. They were:

Peckett 0-4-0ST 'Queen Mary'
Peckett 0-4-0ST No.1378 'Westminster'
Hudswell Clark 0-6-0T No.1069 'Salisbury
Hudswell Clark 0-6-0T No.1070 'Yorkshire'
Hudswell Clark 0-4-0ST No.1045 'Bulford'

There is a photograph but no written record of a Peckett 0-6-0 No.951 saddletank named 'Bristol', and reports that a Sharp Stewart 0-6-0T named 'Sharpness' and a Hawthorn Leslie 0-6-0 named 'Northumbria' also operated on the line at some point.

The line to Lake Down, Stonehenge and Fargo Hospital closed in 1923, with the LMLR finally closing in December 1929. Locomotive No.1378 'Westminster', which was in service from November 1914, is currently in the hands of the Northampton and Lamport Railway, where it is undergoing restoration (opinion is, sadly, that the restoration may never be completed). In 2011, the Stonehenge Landscapes team at the National Trust opened a Geocache trail, featuring the LMLR and the airfields of Lark Hill and RFC Stonehenge.

# 25

# CLOSURE

In pursuance of the powers conferred on me by the Aerial Navigation Acts 1911 and 1913, I hereby make, for the purpose of the safety and defence of the Realm, the following Order: I prohibit the navigation of aircraft of every class and description over the whole area of the United Kingdom, and over the whole of the coastline thereof and territorial waters adjacent thereto. This order shall not apply to Naval and Military aircraft or to aircraft flying under Naval or Military orders, nor shall it apply to any aircraft flying within three miles of a recognised airfield.

R. McKenna, His Majesties Principle Secretary of State.[1]

In the summer of 1914 the Government issued the above order, prohibiting flight across the UK. The final caveat on flight in the vicinity of airfields was a simple expedient aimed at ensuring a supply of fresh pilots through the training system to replace the inevitable casualties on squadrons fighting in Europe. The restriction on flying effectively precluded the establishment of civilian airfields, however, throughout the First World War, the RFC would open several military airfields around Salisbury Plain, at Stonehenge, Lake Down, Old Sarum (Ford Farm), Boscombe Down (Red Farm), Yatesbury and Andover. Military flying at Lark Hill had been winding down since 1913, and when the Bristol Flying School closed on 2 June 1914 it had trained 130 military and civilian pilots, almost half of the total number of qualified pilots in Britain. The site was occupied by an increasingly large number of troops preparing to deploy to France. Two camps of wood and corrugated iron 'Armstrong' huts were built on the flying ground, and young trees were planted in rows around Tombs Road. Despite the size of the task in hand, the efforts of the workforce did not impress Rudyard Kipling who visited the site,

Lark Hill is where the Canadian Engineers live, in the midst of a profligate abundance of tools and carts, pontoon wagons, field telephones, and other mouth-watering gear. Hundreds of tin huts are being built there, but quite leisurely, by contract, I noticed three workmen, at eleven o'clock of that Monday forenoon, as drunk as Davy's sow, reeling and shouting across the landscape. So far as I could ascertain, the workmen do not work extra shifts, nor even, but I hope this is incorrect, on Saturday afternoons; and I think they take their full hour at noon these short days.[2]

Three years later, in 1917, RFC and RNAS personnel based at nearby Stonehenge airfield were billeted at Lark Hill, but contemporary accounts of the accommodation were not favourable. Leslie Semple wrote of the 'awful army huts' in his diary from Stonehenge, 'Moved up into night quarters this afternoon . . . The night mess up here is good – much better than Larkhill'.[3] Many of the huts remained on site until 1966 when major rebuilding works were undertaken at the garrison. The trees around where the flying sheds were located are well-grown and have the appearance of having always been there.

Of the pioneers we have read about, a few went on to attain senior rank in the Royal Air Force, but many, like Lark Hill itself, appear to have faded from memory. Dickson, Barber, Cammell, Cockburn and Loraine have already been discussed. Samuel Cody was killed in a flying accident in 1913. John Capper was promoted out of an aviation job in 1910, then rose to the rank of Major General without any further involvement with aeronautics. Lancelot Gibb was unsuccessful in his attempts to find employment as a civilian pilot and appeared in the bankruptcy courts in 1911. John Fulton gave up flying on leaving CFS and, with George Cockburn, formed the Aeronautical Inspection Department, but died from a throat infection in 1915. John Dunne suffered a complete physical and mental breakdown in 1913 and abandoned aeronautics, he is perhaps better known today for his subsequent work in the field of philosophy. Basil Barrington-Kennett went to France with the RFC, but a loyalty to his old regiment saw him rejoin the Grenadier Guards in 1915, and he was killed whilst leading his company under heavy fire later that summer and was posthumously mentioned in dispatches (B-K was one of three brothers who all lost their lives during the First World War). Bob Allen was killed in a flying accident in 1914 when his biplane crashed at Figheldean, near Netheravon. Alan Fox and Daniel Connor saw action over France, the former was shot down, whilst the latter became an equipment officer early in 1915. Edward Maitland's initial interest was balloons, and he returned to these after breaking both ankles in an aeroplane crash at Lark Hill in 1911. He transferred to the RNAS in 1914, and subsequently to the RAF. Promoted to Air Commodore, he died when the R38 airship broke up in flight in 1921. Collyns Pizey moved from Lark Hill to Bristol Flying School at Brooklands, before joining the RNAS where he was dispatched to Greece to help form the Hellenic Naval Air Service, however, he succumbed to dysentery and died in 1915. Harry Busteed joined the Royal Naval Air Service and served as a Squadron Commander (naval rank) on 'D Flight' (Design Flight) at Eastchurch, and was awarded an OBE in 1918. He became CO of the Marine & Experimental Establishment on the Isle of Grain, and in 1925 was appointed as Senior Fleet Air Arm Officer onboard *HMS Furious*. He came out of retirement during the Second World War and commanded a barrage balloon battery. Lieut Herbert Reynolds served as Staff Officer with the RFC during the First World War before returning to the Royal Engineers. Charles Burke flew with the RFC until 1917, before returning to regimental duties, and was killed in action in 1918. Bayard Hynes decided to give up flying but continued to serve the RFC as an aeroplane engineer.

Today, Larkhill Garrison continues to be the 'Alma Mater' of the Royal Artillery, whose personnel were so instrumental in early aviation on Salisbury Plain. Apart from three helicopter landing sites located there, manned aviation activity has all but ceased; however, it is home for 32 Regiment Royal Artillery who, along with the other regiments in 1 Artillery Brigade, have been responsible to date for operating the Army's unmanned air vehicles (UAVs), such as Phoenix, Desert Hawk Three and Watchkeeper, plus the rotary-wing vehicle Thunder Hawk. The future utilisation of UAVs is likely to be reactive to the theatres they are being used in. British Army systems currently fly surveillance and reconnaissance sorties. However, it is likely that in the future the capabilities of unmanned aircraft, both military and civilian will grow, and their use will become more commonplace. As such, some would say, Larkhill Garrison and the Royal Artillery is playing its part in taking aviation into a new phase, much like it did at the start of the twentieth century.

# Appendix A

## RAeC Certificates awarded at Lark Hill, 1910–14

| No. | Date | Pilot's Name | Aircraft |
|---|---|---|---|
| 27 | 15 Nov 1910 | Capt. J.D.B. Fulton | Henri Farman |
| 32 | 22 Nov 1910 | Mr J.J. Hammond | Bristol Boxkite |
| 45 | 31 Dec 1910 | Lieut R.A. Cammell | " |
| 51 | 24 Jan 1911 | Mr J.H. Thomas | " |
| 54 | 7 Feb 1911 | Lieut D.G. Conner | " |
| 58 | 14 Feb 1911 | Mr G.H. Challenger | " |
| 61 | 14 Feb 1911 | Mr Collyns P. Pizey | " |
| 62 | 14 Feb 1911 | Mr L. Maron | " |
| 69 | 25 Apr 1911 | Mr H.R. Fleming | " |
| 70 | 25 Apr 1911 | Mr Charles C. Turner | " |
| 81 | 9 May 1911 | Mr R.W. Philpott | " |
| 85 | 9 May 1911 | Mr F.P. Raynham | " |
| 87 | 16 May 1911 | Mr E. Hotchkiss | " |
| 92 | 6 Jun 1911 | Lieut H.R.P. Reynolds | " |
| 93 | 13 Jun 1911 | Mr T.H. Sebag-Montefiore | " |
| 94 | 13 Jun 1911 | Mr H.R. Busteed | " |
| 98 | 27 Jun 1911 | Lieut J.W. Pepper | " |
| 112 | 1 Aug 1911 | Mr W. Oswold Watt | " |
| 113 | 1 Aug 1911 | Mr W. Lawrence | " |
| 115 | 17 Aug 1911 | Lieut Col C.O. Smeaton | " |
| 119 | 17 Aug 1911 | Mr Theodore J. Ridge | " |
| 121 | 29 Aug 1911 | Lieut L.V.S. Blacker | " |
| 125 | 29 Aug 1911 | Capt. D. Le G. Pitcher | " |
| 126 | 29 Aug 1911 | Capt. C.G. Hoare | " |
| 129 | 12 Sep 1911 | Mr W.E. Gibson | " |
| 131 | 12 Sep 1911 | Mr E. Harrison | " |

| No. | Date | Pilot's Name | Aircraft |
|-----|------|--------------|----------|
| 132 | 12 Sep 1911 | Mr S.P. Cockerell | Bristol Boxkite |
| 143 | 3 Oct 1911 | Capt. Steele-Hutcheson | " |
| 144 | 3 Oct 1911 | Lieut C.L.N. Newall | " |
| 145 | 10 Oct 1911 | Lieut E.J. Strover | " |
| 148 | 17 Oct 1911 | Mr Zee Hee Lee | " |
| 149 | 24 Oct 1911 | Lieut A.H.A. Hooper | " |
| 150 | 24 Oct 1911 | Lieut E.G.K. Cross | " |
| 155 | 14 Nov 1911 | Mr O.L. Mellersh | " |
| 160 | 28 Nov 1911 | Lieut H.A. Williamson RN | " |
| 161 | 28 Nov 1911 | Mr R. Smith-Barry | " |
| 162 | 28 Nov 1911 | Mr G.B. Dacre | " |
| 163 | 28 Nov 1911 | Lieut J.G. Bower RN | " |
| 169 | 9 Jan 1912 | Lieut G.T. Porter | " |
| 170 | 9 Jan 1912 | Lieut A.E. Borton | " |
| 176 | 30 Jan 1912 | Lieut A.G. Fox | " |
| 177 | 30 Jan 1912 | Lieut E.M. Murray | " |
| 180 | 6 Feb 1912 | Mr W. Bendall | " |
| 185 | 20 Feb 1912 | Lieut B.R.W. Boer | " |
| 191 | 5 Mar 1912 | Lieut C.G.W. Head RN | " |
| 200 | 26 Mar 1912 | Capt. F.J. Brodigan | " |
| 201 | 16 Apr 1912 | Lieut A.E.B. Ashton | " |
| 202 | 16 Apr 1912 | Lieut A.F.A.P. Williams-Freeman RN | " |
| 203 | 16 Apr 1912 | Cdr. O. Schwann RN | " |
| 205 | 16 Apr 1912 | Lieut L.C. Rogers-Harrison | " |
| 206 | 16 Apr 1912 | Sub/Lieut C.H.K. Edmonds RN | " |
| 214 | 14 May 1912 | Lieut A. Hartree | " |
| 220 | 4 Jun 1912 | Mr C.L. Campbell | " |
| 223 | 4 Jun 1912 | Mr M.R.N. Jennings | " |
| 226 | 4 Jun 1912 | Lieut D. Percival | " |
| 234 | 18 Jun 1912 | Lieut Ercole ★ | Bristol Monoplane |
| 241 | 2 Jul 1912 | Maj. L.B. Moss | Bristol Boxkite |
| 249 | 16 Jul 1912 | Lieut K.R. Shaw | " |
| 250 | 16 Jul 1912 | Mr R.A. Lister | " |
| 256 | 24 Jul 1912 | Lieut C.A. Bettington | " |
| 277 | 3 Sep 1912 | Capt. R.H.L. Cordner | " |
| 301 | 17 Sep 1912 | Mr Geoffrey England | " |
| 326 | 15 Oct 1912 | Mr A.V. Bettington | Bristol Monoplane |
| 327 | 15 Oct 1912 | Capt. R.S.H. Grace | Bristol Boxkite |
| 332 | 15 Oct 1912 | Mr H.W. Hall | Bristol Monoplane |
| 347 | 29 Oct 1912 | Lieut G.A. Parker | Bristol Boxkite |
| 348 | 29 Oct 1912 | Capt. J.L. Lucen | " |

| No. | Date | Pilot's Name | Aircraft |
|---|---|---|---|
| 356 | 12 Nov 1912 | Capt. O. de L. Williams | Bristol Boxkite |
| 357 | 12 Nov 1912 | Capt. H. Musgrave | " |
| 363 | 12 Nov 1912 | Capt. F.G. Kunhardt | " |
| 366 | 26 Nov 1912 | Lieut C.G. MacArthur RN | " |
| 367 | 26 Nov 1912 | Prince Serge Cantacuzene | Bristol Monoplane |
| 370 | 17 Dec 1912 | Mid. N.F. Wheeler RN | Bristol Boxkite |
| 376 | 17 Dec 1912 | Mr V.P. Taylor | " |
| 383 | 7 Jan 1913 | Lieut G. Negresco ★ | Bristol Monoplane |
| 396 | 21 Jan 1913 | Sub/Lieut A.W.R. Bigsworth RNR | Bristol Boxkite |
| 397 | 21 Jan 1913 | Lieut F.W. Bowhill RNR | " |
| 403 | 21 Jan 1913 | Sub/Lieut R.L.G. Marix RNR | " |
| 404 | 21 Jan 1913 | Lieut H.D. Vernon RN | " |
| 405 | 21 Jan 1913 | Sub/Lieut H.A. Littleton RNVR | " |
| 417 | 18 Feb 1913 | 2nd Lieut R.M. Vaughan | " |
| 463 | 12 Apr 1913 | 2nd Lieut W.R. Reid | " |
| 466 | 23 Apr 1913 | Mr H.C. Lower | " |
| 470 | 30 Apr 1913 | 2nd Lieut R. Marshall | " |
| 471 | 30 Apr 1913 | 2nd Lieut M.R. Chidson | " |
| 481 | 13 May 1913 | Lieut F.G. Brodbribb RN | " |
| 508 | 3 Jun 1913 | Capt. G.M. Griffith | " |
| 511 | 12 Jun 1913 | Mr. J.R. de Laplane | " |
| 513 | 13 Jun 1913 | Mr G.L. Gipps | " |
| 514 | 13 Jun 1913 | Mr F.P. Adams | " |
| 516 | 13 Jun 1913 | Lieut R. Burns | " |
| 518 | 14 Jun 1913 | Lieut E.O. Priestley RN | " |
| 528 | 21 Jun 1913 | Capt. A. Popovicz ★ | " |
| 532 | 30 Jun 1913 | Lieut Col A.B. Hamilton | " |
| 533 | 1 Jul 1913 | Lieut A.J. Miley RN | " |
| 536 | 1 Jul 1913 | Lieut E. Osmond RN | " |
| 539 | 2 Jul 1913 | Capt. A.C. Barmby RMLI | " |
| 540 | 2 Jul 1913 | Lieut R.E. Orton | " |
| 542 | 4 Jul 1913 | Lieut C. Beroniade ★ | Bristol Monoplane |
| 543 | 4 Jul 1913 | Lieut A. Pacanu ★ | " |
| 553 | 11 Jul 1913 | 2nd Lieut J.H.M. Stevenson | Bristol Boxkite |
| 590 | 14 Aug 1913 | Surg. Lt. F.G. Hitch RN | " |
| 599 | 20 Aug 1913 | Capt. C.F. Murphy | " |
| 600 | 21 Aug 1913 | 2nd Lieut O.G.W.G. Lywood | " |
| 602 | 26 Aug 1913 | 2nd Lieut B.M.B. Bateman | " |
| 605 | 28 Aug 1913 | Lieut Lord G. Wellesley | " |
| 612 | 30 Aug 1913 | Capt. B.D. Fisher | " |
| 613 | 30 Aug 1913 | The Hon. F.W.L. Vernon | " |

| No. | Date | Pilot's Name | Aircraft |
|-----|------|-------------|----------|
| 618 | 10 Sep 1913 | Mr W.H.S. Garnett | Bristol Monoplane |
| 620 | 11 Sep 1913 | Lieut N.M. Jenkins | Bristol Boxkite |
| 635 | 22 Sep 1913 | Capt. F.A. Ferguson | " |
| 650 | 15 Oct 1913 | Herr W. Voigt | " |
| 657 | 22 Oct 1913 | Capt. G.C.B. Buckland | " |
| 662 | 24 Oct 1913 | Lieut A. Gallaher | " |
| 663 | 24 Oct 1913 | Lieut K.F.W. Dunn | " |
| 682 | 8 Nov 1913 | 2nd Lieut M.W. Huish | " |
| 688 | 21 Nov 1913 | 2nd Lieut W.R.E. Harrison | " |
| 689 | 22 Nov 1913 | Mr H.S.N. Courtney | " |
| 694 | 26 Nov 1913 | Lieut A.C.E. Marsh | " |
| 702 | 11 Dec 1913 | Capt. B.H.L. Hay | " |
| 718 | 24 Dec 1913 | Lieut R.C. Halahan RN | " |
| 742 | 25 Feb 1914 | Mr W.J. Stutt | " |
| 756 | 26 Mar 1914 | Lieut A.S. Barratt | " |
| 758 | 27 Mar 1914 | Capt. E.A.H. Fell | " |
| 761 | 3 Apr 1914 | Lieut A.K.D. George | " |
| 762 | 15 Apr 1914 | 2nd Lieut J.B. Bolitho | " |
| 764 | 15 Apr 1914 | 2nd Lieut J.B. Harman | " |
| 771 | 21 Apr 1914 | Lieut P.S. Myburgh | " |
| 775 | 28 Apr 1914 | Air Mech. A.J. Locker | " |

## Notes:

1.  Certificates Nos 1-452 bore the date of the RAeC Committee meeting when the Certificate was awarded, not the date of the test flight. Several of those awarded in 1910 had passed their test the previous year, but from 1911 onwards it may be assumed that the date of the test was 7–14 days prior to the award of the certificate.

2.  From Certificate No. 453 onwards the award was backdated to the date of the test.

3.  Foreign service pilots are marked ★

# Appendix B

❧

## Competitors in the Circuit of Britain Air Race, 1911

### *Order of Departure*

1.   **Lieut Conneau aka 'André Beaumont' (France) Blériot**
2.   Mr Henry J.D. Astley (Britain) Birdling monoplane
3.   *Maj. Brindejonc des Moulinais (France) Morane-Borel*
4.   *Mr R.C. Fenwick (Britain) Handley Page*
5.   Lieut John C. Porte RN (Britain) Deperdussin
6.   *Mr Ronald C. Kemp (Britain) Avro*
7.   Mr Cecil Compton-Paterson (Britain) Grahame–White Baby
8.   *Mr O.C. Morison (Britain) Bristol Prier*
9.   **Maj. Jules Védrines (France) Morane–Borel**
10.  *Mr James Radley (Britain) Antoinette*
11.  Maj. G. Blanchet (France) Breguet biplane
12.  Lieut Reginald A. Cammell (Britain) Blériot XXI
13.  Herr Edmond Audemars (Germany) Blériot
14.  **Mr James 'Jimmy' Valentine (Britain) Deperdussin**
15.  *Mr Douglas Graham-Gilmour (Britain) Bristol*
16.  Mr E.C. Gordon England (Britain) Bristol T Type
17.  Mr Collyns P. Pizey (Britain) Bristol T Type
18.  *Pierre Prier (France) Bristol Prier*
19.  Mr C. Howard Pixton (Britain) Bristol T Type
20.  **Mr Samuel Cody (USA) Cody III biplane**
21.  *Maj. M. Tabateau (France) Bristol*
22.  Mr F. Conway Jenkins (Britain) Blackburn monoplane
23.  Maj. Olivier de Montalent (France) Breguet biplane
24.  Mr Gustav Hamel (Britain) Blériot
25.  Lieut Henry R.P. Reynolds (Britain) Howard Wright
26.  *Mr Robert Loraine (Britain) Nieuport*

27.    Mr Bentfield Charles 'Benny' Hucks (Britain) Blackburn monoplane
28.    Mr Charles T. Weymann (American) Nieuport
29.    Hern Jann Wijnmalen (The Netherlands) Henri Farman
30.    Lieut H. Bier (Austria) Etrich monoplane

## Note:

The Bristol Prier monoplanes (Entry Nos 15 and 18) did not compete. Prier crashed his machine on the morning of the race, whilst Graham-Gilmour was suspended by the RAeC for dangerous flying over the University Boat Race, and was therefore unable to start. Other non-starters are shown in italics. The four pilots to complete the course are shown in bold type.

# APPENDIX C

Entrants for the Military Trials, 1912

| Ser | Name (Engine fitted) |
|-----|----------------------|
| 1. | Hanriot monoplane (100hp Gnome) Pilot: J. Bielovucic |
| 2. | Hanriot monoplane (100hp Gnome) Pilot: Sydney Sippe |
| 3. | Vickers No.6 monoplane (70hp Viale) Pilot: Leslie F. MacDonald |
| 4. | Blériot XI-2 monoplane (70hp Gnome) Pilot: Edmond Perreyon |
| 5. | Blériot XXI monoplane (70hp Gnome) Pilot: Edmond Perreyon |
| 6.★ | Avro Type G biplane (60hp Green) Pilot: – |
| 7. | Avro Type G biplane (60hp ABC) Pilot: Lieut W. Parke RN |
| 8.★ | Breguet U2 biplane (110hp Canton-Unné) Pilot: René Moineau |
| 9.★ | Breguet U2 biplane (110hp Canton-Unné) Pilot: W.B. Rhodes-Moorhouse |
| 10.★ | Coventry Ordnance Works biplane (100hp Gnome) Pilot: Tom Sopwith |
| 11.★ | Coventry Ordnance Works biplane (100hp Chenu) Pilot: Tom Sopwith |
| 12. | Bristol G.E.2 biplane (100hp Gnome) Pilot: Gordon England |
| 13. | Bristol G.E.2 biplane (70hp Daimler-Mercedes) Pilot: Howard Pixton |
| 14. | Bristol-Coanda monoplane (80hp Gnome) Pilot: Harry Busteed |
| 15. | Bristol-Coanda monoplane (80hp Gnome) Pilot: James Valentine / H.Pixton |
| 16.★ | Flanders biplane (100hp ABC) Pilot: Frederick P. Raynham |
| 17. | Martin-Handasyde monoplane (75hp Chenu) Pilot: Gordon Bell |
| 18.★ | Aerial Wheel (50hp NEC) Pilot: Cecil Pashley |
| 19. | Mersey monoplane (45hp Isaacson) Pilot: Robert C. Fenwick |
| 20. | Deperdussin monoplane (100hp Anzani) Pilot: Lieut John C. Porte RN |
| 21. | Deperdussin monoplane (100hp Gnome) Pilot: Jules Védrines |
| 22. | Maurice Farman biplane (70hp Renault) Pilot: Pierre Verrier |
| 23.★ | D.F.W. Mars monoplane (100hp Mercedes) Pilot: Lieut Bier |
| 24.★ | Lohner biplane (120hp Austro-Daimler) Pilot: Lieut von Blaschke |
| 25.★ | Harper monoplane (60hp Green) Pilot: – |
| 26. | Deperdussin monoplane (100hp Gnome) Pilot: Maurice Prévost |

27.★    Deperdussin monoplane (100hp Gnome) Pilot: Maurice Prévost
28.★    Handley Page Type F monoplane (70hp Gnome) Pilot: Henry Petre
29.★    Piggott biplane (35hp Anzani) Pilot: S.C. Parr
30.★    Cody IV monoplane (120hp Austo-Daimler) Pilot: –
31.      Cody V biplane 'Cathedral' (120hp Austro-Daimler) Pilot: Samuel Cody
32.★    Borel Monoplane (80hp Gnome) Pilot: Chambenois

## Notes:

1.  Military Aeroplane Competition was the title used by the Government, however, most sources, contemporary and otherwise, have referred to this event as the Military Trials.
2.  Robert Fenwick (19) was killed when his Mersey monoplane crashed during the Trials
3.  Nos 20 and 21. Some early accounts transpose the identities of the two British-built Deperdussins. The serial numbers shown are the majority presentation.
4.  The Avro Type (7) arrived at Lark Hill with No. 6's Green engine fitted, as the ABC engine was not ready.
5.★ Entrants which did not compete in the Trials.

# Appendix D

## Royal Flying Corps Personnel, 1914

| | |
|---|---|
| Commandant: | **Maj. Sir Alexander Bannerman RE** |
| Adjutant: | **Capt. P.W.L. Broke-Smith RE** |
| Experimental Officer: | **Capt. A.D. Carden RE** |
| Quatermaster: | **Lieut (QM) F.H. Kirby VC** |

### No. I Company – Farnborough

| | |
|---|---|
| Commanding Officer No.1 Co. | Capt. E.M. Maitland Essex Regt |
| | **Lieut A.G. Fox RE** (transferred to No.2 Co after Cammell's death) |
| | **Lieut C.M. Waterlow RE** |
| | **2nd Lieut J.N. Fletcher RE** |
| | Capt. C.R.W. Allen |
| | Lieut G.E. Manisty 67th Punjabis |
| Commanding Officer No.2 Co. | Capt. J.H.B. Fulton RFA |
| | Capt. E.B. Loraine Grenadier Guards |
| | Capt. Brooke-Popham Ox & Bucks LI |
| | Capt. S.D. Massey 29th Punjabis |
| | Capt. F.H. Sykes 15th Hussars |
| | Capt. C.J. Burke Royal Irish |
| | Lieut G.B. Hynes RA |
| | Lieut B.H. Barrington-Kennett Grenadier Guards |
| | **Lieut R. Cammell RE** |
| | Lieut D.G. Conner RFA |
| | **Lieut H.R.P. Reynolds RE** |

*Note:*
1. Royal Engineer Officers are shown in bold
2. Lieut R.T. Snowden-Smith ASC was posted to Air Battalion (Flight May 1911) but there is no record of his actually having served.

### The Aircraft Factory – Farnborough

| | |
|---|---|
| Superintendent: | Mr Mervyn O'Goram |

| | | |
|---|---|---|
| Air Battalion Other Ranks | CSM Ramsay | Spr Osborne |
| | SSgt Wilson | Spr Green |
| | CS McAllister | Spr Garner |
| | Cpl Slade | Spr Langton |
| | LCpl Brockbank | Spr Evans |
| | LCpl Jeffery | Spr Traylor |
| | 2Cpl Ridd | Spr Keszler |
| | Spr Breading | Spr Roberts |
| | Spr Mullens | Spr Geard |
| Special Reserve | LWF Turner | RH Carr |
| | CFM Chambers | |
| | FG Dunne | |

# The Officers of the Royal Flying Corps, 1912

### The Central Flying School

| | |
|---|---|
| Commandant: | Capt. Godfrey Payne MVO RN |
| Deputy Commandant & Instructor in Theory & Construction: | Lieut Col H.R. Cook |
| Staff Officer: | Maj. H.M. Trenchard DSO |
| Secretary: | Asst Paymaster J.N. Lidderdale RN |
| Flying Instructors: | Maj. E.L. Gerrard RM |
| | Capt. J.D.B. Fulton |
| | Capt. P.W.L. Broke-Smith |
| | Lieut A.M. Longmore RN |
| Inspector of Engines: | Eng-Lieut C.J.R. Randall RN |
| Quartermaster: | Hon. Lieut F.H. Kirby VC |

### The Military Wing

| | |
|---|---|
| Commandant: | Maj. F.H. Sykes |
| Deputy Commandant: | Maj. W.E.S. Burch |
| Adjutant: | Lieut B.H. Barrington-Kennett |

### No.1 Squadron

| | |
|---|---|
| Squadron Commander: | Maj. E M Maitland |

### No.2 Squadron

| | |
|---|---|
| Squadron Commander: | Maj. C.J. Burke |

| Flight Commanders: | Capt. G.H. Raleigh |
| | Capt. H.R.P. Reynolds |
| Flying Officers: | Capt. G.W.P. Dawes |
| | Lieut C.A.H. Longcroft |
| | Lieut G.B. Haynes |
| | Lieut G.T. Porter |
| | Lieut C.T. Carfrae |

## No.3 Squadron

| Squadron Commander: | Maj. H.R.M. Brooke-Popham |
| Flight Commanders: | Capt. C.R.W. Allen |
| | Capt. B.R.W. Beor |
| | Capt. D.G. Conner |
| | Flying Officer: Lieut A.G. Fox |

## Naval Wing

| Officer Commanding: | Cdr C.R. Samson RN |
| Flying Officers: | Capt. R. Gordon RM |
| | Lieut J.W. Sneddon RN |
| | Lieut W. Parke RN |
| | Lieut C.J. L'Estrange-Malone RN |
| | Sub/Lieut F.E.T. Hewlett RN |

## Reserve

| Commandant: | Brig. Gen. D.C.B. Henderson DSO |
| | C (Dir Mil Trg) |
| Assistant: | Lieut Gordon Bell |
| Special Reserve: | R.L. Charteris |
| | R.O. Abercromby |
| | D. Corbett-Wilson |
| | T. O'B Hubbard |
| | H.D. Cutler |
| | D.G. Young |
| | R.R. Smith-Barry |
| | W.E. Gibson |
| | M.R.N. Jennings |
| | C.P. Pizey |
| | G. de Havilland |

## Royal Aircraft Factory, Farnborough

| Superintendent: | Mr Mervyn O'Gorman |

*Note:*

1.  No.1 Squadron was responsible for kites, balloons and airships. Although No.2 and 3
    Squadrons were officially based at Lark Hill, No.2 Squadron actually operated from
    Farnborough, and the Naval Wing was stationed at RNAS Eastchurch.

2.  Lieuts S.D.A. Grey and R.H. Clark RN joined Naval Wing soon after this list was
    published, as did the Inspector of Aircraft, Capt. F.R. Scarlett RN.

    Names of many RFC WOs & SNCOs are given below the Corps photographs in
    Appendix F.

# APPENDIX E

Aeroplanes believed to have been at Lark Hill, 1909–14

### Aeronautical Syndicate Ltd Monoplane No.2
–       Flying trials 02/10

### Aeronautical Syndicate Ltd Valkyrie
–       Flying trials 10/10 then production moved to Hendon

### Avro 500 Type Es
No.285   No.3 Sqn Lark Hill -/13
No.288   No.3 Sqn Lark Hill -/13
No.289   No.3 Sqn Lark Hill -/13
No.290   No.3 Sqn Lark Hill -/13
No.291   No.3 Sqn Lark Hill -/13
No.404   From CFS Upavon (flown by Lieut Smith-Barry)
No.405   From CFS Upavon (flown by Cdr. Samson RN)

### Avro Type G
–       Military Trials Lark Hill (No.7) during 08/12

### Blériot XI
–       Unregistered bought by Capt. Fulton. Lark Hill 07/10. Air Battalion by 03/11
         until 11/05/12
–       'Beaumont' Circuit of Britain Air Race 26/07/11
No.219   From No.2 Sqn at Farnborough to No.3 Sqn Lark Hill 21/06/13. To CFS
         Upavon 27/10/13
No.221   Military Trials Lark Hill (No.4) 08/12, RFC No.3 Sqn 09/12 to Netheravon
         -/13

## Blériot XII

B1      Air Battalion 'Man Killer' donated by Laycock/Westminster arrived Lark Hill 09/10/10 to Farnborough by 04/01/11

## Blériot XXI

B2      Lieut Cammell 22/05/11 to Farnborough 02/12. RFC No.3 Sqn No.251 10/12. Disposed 20/12/13

–      Military Trials Lark Hill (No.5) during 08/12

## Bregeut L1 Biplane

B3      Air Battalion 10/11 No.202

–      Military Trials Lark Hill (No.8) during 08/12

## Bristol Standard Biplane 'Boxkite'

No.7      Trials Lark Hill 30/07/10 to Lanark 08/10 Gregoiré 40/50hp engine

No.8      Lark Hill 09/10 flown by Loraine during Manœuvres ENV 8 Cylinder 60hp engine

No.9      Lark Hill 09/10 flown By Dickson during Manouevres. Sent to India

No.12      Bristol Flying School Lark Hill. Arrived from India 1911. Damaged by Smith-Barry 10/11

No.14      Bristol Flying School Lark Hill

No.19      Lark Hill to Brooklands 05/13

No. 37      Air Battalion Lark Hill 18/05/11

No.38      Air Battalion F4 Lark Hill 25/05/11

No.39      Air Battalion F6 Lark Hill 09/07/11 Renault 60hp engine (modified with nacelle in front of pilot)

No.40      Air Battalion F5 Lark Hill 31/07/11 non-flying spare airframe (upper wing extensions)

No.41      Air Battalion Lark Hill 31/07/11 non-flying spare airframe

No.42      Air Battalion F7 Lark Hill 02/08/11 Renault 60hp engine, RFC No.408

No.43      Bristol Flying School Lark Hill

No.48      Air Battalion Lark Hill 08/11

No.49      Air Battalion Lark Hill 08/11

No.66      Bristol Flying School Lark Hill 01/12

No.69      Bristol Flying School. Built as racing machine, modified by Voisin. Lark Hill 02/12 crashed 03/11/12

## Bristol Challenger-Grandseigne Racing Biplane

No.33      Lark Hill 04/11 wrecked by Grandseigne during initial flight test

## Bristol Challenger-Low Monoplane

No.35      Lark Hill 02/11 to Filton 04/11 prior to Olympia Show

### Bristol Biplane T Type / Challenger-Dickson Biplane

No.45     Larkhill flown by Tetard

No.51     Larkhill Circuit of Britain Air Race 07/11 to be flown by Graham-Gilmour
          (did not compete)

No.52     Bristol Flying School Lark Hill 06/11 flown by Collyns Pizey in the Circuit of
          Britain, sold 22/07/11

No.53     Larkhill Circuit of Britain Air Race 07/11 flown by Gordon England

No.54     Larkhill Circuit of Britain Air Race 07/11 flown by Howard Pixton

### Bristol Biplane T Type / Challenger-England Biplane

No.59     Bristol Flying School Lark Hill 11/11 crashed & dismantled 06/12

### Bristol Prier Monoplane

No.46     P-1 Bristol Aeroplane Co. Trials July 1911

No.58     Bristol Flying School Lark Hill 10/11 crashed 30/10/11, repaired and flying at
          Lark Hill during 1912

No.73     Bristol Flying School Lark Hill 11/11

No.75     Air Battalion B6 Lark Hill 17/02/12 crashed 26/04/12. Modified as Prier-
          Dickson RFC No.256 Capt. Allen. To Farnborough 28/03/13

### Bristol Prier-Dickson Monoplane

No.82     Lark Hill 27/07/12 sent to Spain

No.91     3 Sqn RFC Lark Hill No.261 17/09/12. To Farnborough struck off 05/08/13

No.97     Bristol Flying School Lark Hill 05/12 crashed 06/12

No.98     Bristol Flying School Lark Hill 06/12

No.102    Bristol Flying School Lark Hill 11/12 crashed 18/07/13

### Bristol Gordon England Biplane G.E.1

No.64     Trials Lark Hill 07/12 sold to Germany, returned scrapped 09/12

### Bristol Gordon England Biplane G.E.2

No.103    Gnome 100hp radial engine Military Trials Lark Hill (No.12) during 08/12

No.104    Daimler-Mercedes 70hp in-line water-cooled engine Military Trials Lark Hill
          (No.13) during 08/12

### Bristol Coanda Monoplane Single-Seat

No.77     Trials Lark Hill 27/03/12

No.105    Military Trials Lark Hill (No.14) 08/12 bought by WO No.263 crashed
          10/09/12

No.106    Military Trials Lark Hill (No.15) 08/12 bought by WO No.262

No.111    'The Elephant' Trials at Lark Hill 09/12 Daimler-Mercedes engine. Intended
          for Deutsche Bristol Werke. Never flew.

No.121   Purchase by Italian Government cancelled, Lark Hill BFS 10/12. Filton for overhaul 02/13 converted to TB8.

No.143   Trials Lark Hill

No.144   Trials Lark Hill (to RNAS Eastchurch converted to TB8 Hydroplane 08/13)

No.146   Rumania Geoffrey England killed during acceptance test flight crash 05/03/13

## Bristol Coanda Monoplane Side-by-side

No.80    Bristol Flying School Lark Hill 05/12 crashed Merriam 26/01/14

No.177   Bristol Flying School Lark Hill converted from single-seat as No.218. Converted TB8 Biplane.

## Bristol Coanda Type BR7

No.157   Trials Lark Hill flown by Pixton 03/13

No.158   Trials Lark Hill 26/05/13 flown by Pizey with Fellowes as passenger when carburettor caught fire. Destroyed.

No.160   BFS Larkhill 05/13 rarely flown

No.161   BFS Larkhill 05/13 rarely flown

No.162   BFS Larkhill 05/13 rarely flown

No.163   BFS Larkhill 05/13 rarely flown, tested with two-wheel Vee landing gear

## Bristol TB8

No.121   Trials Lark Hill 07/13 flown by Pixton and Jullerot to RNAS at Dale 20/09/13

## Bristol Coanda Type GB75

No.223   Trials Lark Hill 07/04/14 Rumanian order cancelled 06/14

## Bristol S.S.A (Single-seat Armoured) Biplane

Initial trials 08/05/14 flown by Sippé

## Bristol 'Baby' Scout

No.206   Trials Lark Hill 23/02/14 returned to Filton 04/14

No.219   Trials Lark Hill 08/05/14 returned to Filton 25/06/14

## Carter Biplane

–        Private trials at Lark Hill 01/11

## Cockburn Biplane

–        Private trials Lark Hill 11/01/12

## Cody III Biplane

–        Circuit of Britain Air Race 26/07/11

## Cody V 'Catherdral' Biplane
–       Military Trials Lark Hill (No.31) 08/12 RFC No.301

## Coventry Ordnance Works Biplane
–       Military Trials Lark Hill (No.10) during 08/12
–       Military Trials Lark Hill (No.11) during 08/12

## Deperdussin Monoplane
–       Valentine Circuit of Britain Air Race 26/07/11
B5      Air Battalion Lark Hill 20/01/12 RFC No.252 struck off 26/11/13
–       Bought by Capt Hamilton. RFC 06/12 RFC No.257 struck off 26/11/13
–       Military Trials Lark Hill (No.20) during 08/12 Anzani 100hp engine
–       Military Trials Lark Hill (No.21) 08/12 Gnome 100hp engine RFC 27/10/12
        No.259 to Farnborough 25/01/13
–       Military Trials Lark Hill (No.26) 08/12 RFC No.258

## Dunne-Capper Monoplane
–       Private trials at Lark Hill 01/11 (Col Capper and Lieut Cammell)

## Dunne D8 Biplane
–       Military Trials (non-competing) 08/12

## Handley Page Type F HP.6
–       Military Trials Lark Hill (No.28) during 08/12

## Hanriot Monoplane
–       Military Trials Lark Hill (No.1) during 08/12
–       Military Trials Lark Hill (No.2) during 08/12

## Henri Farman III 'Type Militaire'
F1      Air Battalion Lark Hill 06/11 last flight at Lark Hill 10/06/12. To CFS Upavon
        as an instructional airframe.

## Henri Farman F20
No.274  RFC No.3 Sqn Lark Hill 06/13
No.277  RFC No.3 Sqn Lark Hill 06/13
No.284  RFC No.3 Sqn Lark Hill 10/04/13
No.286  RFC No.3 Sqn Lark Hill 06/13

## Howard Wright Biplane
–       Owned by Capt. Maitland Lark Hill sold to Air Battalion No.F3 23/06/11,
        engine failure 08/07/11. Rebuilt by Royal Aircraft Factory as BE.6 No.206.

### Martin-Handasyde Monoplane
– Military Trials Lark Hill (No.17) 08/12 RFC No.278

### Maurice Farman Coupe Michelin (Racing Machine)
– Great Autumn Manœuvres 09/10 Lieut L. Gibbs (type not confirmed)

### Maurice Farman S.7 'Longhorn' Biplane
– Military Trials Lark Hill (No.22) during 08/12
No.214 Air Battalion Lark Hill 04/11
No.216 No.3 Sqn RFC Lark Hill 06/13 crashed en-route to Lydd 20/07/13
No.270 Battalion Lark Hill 06/13

### Maurice Farman S.11 'Shorthorn' Biplane
No.369 No.3 Sqn RFC Lark Hill 06/13

### Mersey Monoplane
– Military Trials Lark Hill (No.19) 08/12 crashed Fenwick killed 13/08/12

### Morane-Borel
– Circuit of Britain Air Race 26/07/11 Védrines

### Nieuport
B4 Air Battalion Lark Hill 09/11 RFC 05/12 No.253 sent to Farnborough 14/03/13

### Nieuport Type IVG
– Unregistered. Crashed by E. Loraine on acceptance trials at Lark Hill 05/07/12
No.254 No.3 Sqn Lark Hill 02/08/12 damaged 14/08/12 returned after repair at Farnborough.
No.255 No.3 Sqn Lark Hill. No record of having flown. Returned to Farnborough 15/02/13.

### Nieuport Type IIN
No.264 No.3 Sqn Lark Hill 22/10/12. Returned to Farnborough 01/02/13

### Paulhan Biplane
F2 After tests and repair at Farnborough to Air Battalion 10/11. Dismantled 12/11 and sent back to Farnborough 03/02/12 without having flown.

### Piggott Biplane
– Military Trials Lark Hill (No.29) 08/12 retired from the trials 25/08/12

## *Royal Aircraft Factory BE1*

B1        Trials Lark Hill 11/03/12. No.2 Co Air Battalion. Passed onto No.2 Squadron
          RFC as 201

## *Royal Aircraft Factory BE2/2a*

–         Military Trials Lark Hill (Non-competing) 08/08/12 – 14/08/12
No.205   RFC Farnborough 06/13 (formerly B.E.5)
No.272   RFC (probably No.2 Sqn) date unknown

## *Royal Aircraft Factory BE3*

No.203   'The Goldfish' No.3 Sqn 28/05/12 mod 03/14 remained at Farnborough as
          training airframe (allegedly reconstructed from Paulhan F2)

## *Royal Aircraft Factory BE4*

No.204   No.3 Sqn crashed at Netheravon 11/03/14

## *Royal Aircraft Factory FE2*

–         Military Trials Lark Hill (Non-competing) 08/12, fitted with maxim gun.

## *Short School Biplane S.32/43*

No. 401  (or 402) Fm CFS Upavon. Lieut Longmore RN 07/11

## *Vickers REP Monoplane*

–         Trials Lark Hill 03/12

## *Vickers No.6 Monoplane*

–         Military Trials Lark Hill (No.3) during 08/12

**Note:**

This aircraft listing is not the result of academic research but is intended to provide an indication
of the variety of aircraft flown from Lark Hill, and the tasks undertaken there.

# APPENDIX F

## RFC photographs, 1914

Officers of the Royal Flying Corps, outside Netheravon Officers' Mess (still standing):
**Front Row L to R**: Capt. Beatty, Capt. Dawes, Maj. Hon. C. Brabazon, Maj. Musgrave, Maj. Raleigh, Maj. Higgins, Lieut Col Sykes, Lieut Barrington-Kennett, Capt. Conner, Capt. Cholmondley, Capt. Herbert, Capt. Charlton, Capt. Carmichael.
**2nd Row**: Capt. Holt, Capt. Shephard, Capt. Grey, Capt. Stopford, Capt. Beor, Capt. Todd, Capt. Waldron, Lieut Hynes, Lieut Mills, Lieut Joubert de la Ferte, Lieut Fuller.
**3rd Row**: Lieut Smith, Lieut Christie, Lieut Stodart, Lieut Rodwell, Lieut James, Lieut Spence, Lieut Mansfield, Lieut Humphreys, Lieut Gould, Lieut Mitchell, Lieut Cogan, Lieut R. Small, Lieut Allen, Lieut Pryce.
**4th Row**: Lieut Penn-Gaskell, Lieut Dawes, Lieut Martyn, Lieut Vaughan, Lieut Birch, Lieut Read, Lieut Adams, Lieut Borton, Lieut Corballis, Lieut Mapplebeck.
**5th Row**: Lieut Harvey-Kelly, Lieut Freeman, Lieut McNeece, Lieut Glanville, Lieut Noel, Lieut Wadham, Lieut Porter, Lieut Playfair, Lieut Hubbard, Lieut Lewis, Lieut Morgan, Lieut F. Small.
**6th Row**: Lieut Mansergh, Lieut Carpenter, Lieut Shekelton, Lieut Atkinson, Lieut Hartree, Lieut Moore, Lieut Hoskins, Lieut Waterfall, Lieut Lywood, Lieut Hordern.
Warrant Officers of the Royal Flying Corps, June 1914

**Front Row L to R**: Sgt-Maj. Thomas, Sgt-Maj. Parker, Sgt-Maj. Ramsey, Col Sykes (CO), Sgt-Maj. Fletcher, Sgt-Maj. Measures, Sgt-Maj. Starling.
**2nd Row**: Sgt-Maj. Wilford, F.Sgt Lacy, F.Sgt Brockbank, F.Sgt Hilliar, F.Sgt Jillings, F.Sgt Bruce, F.Sgt Ridd, F.Sgt Carter, F.Sgt Nicholls, Sgt-Maj. Unwin.

Royal Flying Corps SNCOs, June 1914. (*Flight*)

# APPENDIX G

━━◦

## Formation of the RAF, 1918

The world's first independent air force was formed on 1 April 1918. Whilst not directly relevant to the story of aviation on Salisbury Plain, readers will perhaps excuse a short examination of this key point in British military aviation history as a conclusion to this story. Ever since the creation of the RFC, the Admiralty and the War Office had not really seen eye-to-eye on aviation matters. The government established an Air Committee in 1912 to act as an intermediary, but this was not particularly effective. At the outbreak of the First World War, the RFC deployed to France with the British Expeditionary Force, and the task of air defence of Great Britain was left to the RNAS. But the Admiralty was focusing on the development of seaplanes and aviation ships to defend our coastal waters; constantly being reminded by the RFC that home defence was a role they would take back in due course.

Although the Admiralty was perhaps slightly more generous in funding the naval wing than the War Office was with Military Wing, in the early years of the First World War neither fighting arm was particularly well equipped with either quality or quantity of assets. The Germans, on the other hand, had the advantage, and with large numbers of aeroplanes and fast, high flying Zeppelins they began to launch raids on British cities. In an attempt not to give away intelligence of how successful these raids had been, the British Government chose not to publish the details of casualties. Although the number of deaths was relatively small, the public outcry at the audacity of such attacks was immense and the British public assumed the death toll was high. Despite the fact that it was the Zeppelin threat which inspired formation of the RFC in the first place, during the early years of conflict, the War Office focused on the use of aeroplanes for reconnaissance, whilst the Admiralty wanted a more aggressive and strategic role for their aviators. The disagreement was tolerated for a while, but faced with the Zeppelin raids a more concerted effort by the RNAS and RFC was demanded, and in 1916 the Joint War Air Committee was formed under the chairmanship of Lord Derby, to take over where previous groups had failed. But it lacked any executive powers and was equally ineffective. After just eight meetings Derby resigned, saying, 'It appears to me quite impossible to bring the two wings together... unless and until the whole system of the Air Service is changed and they are amalgamated into one service.'

The following May, the Air Board was created and, comprising cabinet ministers and other political figures, it was hoped it would have more effect; however, in its first report it stated, 'Although the Army authorities were ready and willing to take part in meetings, the Navy were often absent from Board meetings and frequently refused to provide information on naval aviation.' To help address this, senior naval officers were appointed onto the Air Board, including Godfrey Paine who was now Director of Naval Aviation. However, the problems with the British air defence was a national issue that the Prime Minister, David Lloyd-George, had to address. He met with General Jan Smuts and David Henderson to resolve the matter, and on 24 August 1917 Smuts wrote in his report to the War Cabinet, 'The day may not be far off when aerial operations . . . may become the principal operations of war, to which the older forms of military and naval operations may be secondary and subordinate', and he recommended a new service be formed that would be equal to the Royal Navy and the Army, and receive direction from the Air Ministry. In an eleventh hour demonstration of unity, Admiral Beatty (First Sea Lord), Field Marshall Haig and Maj. Gen. Hugh Trenchard (Commander of the RFC in France) all expressed their opposition to the merger. Haig and Trenchard wrote to Field Marshall Sir William Robertson (Chief of the Imperial General Staff), but the political weight of a relatively small number of civilian deaths in London far outweighed the much greater, but out-of-sight, losses on the Western Front, and their protests were to no avail. The Air Force (Constitution) Act was presented to Parliament on 8 November and received royal assent on 29 November 1917.

Despite being reluctant to leave the Western Front, and vehement opposition from Haig who did not want to lose his right-hand man, Trenchard was appointed to the Air Ministry as Chief of the Air Staff in December 1917. He reluctantly took up the post and later said of the decision, 'A more gigantic waste of effort and personnel there has never been in any war'. Trenchard worked for the Secretary of State for Air, Lord Rothermere, whom he thought was too concerned with political intrigue as opposed to concentrating his efforts on what was happening in France. When Rothermere informed the Admiralty they would be getting 4,000 aeroplanes, which did not exist, Trenchard tended his resignation on 19 March 1918, and his place was taken by Maj. Gen. Frederick Sykes (who had been the first commanding officer of the Military Wing of the RFC in 1912). Trenchard was immediately summoned to Buckingham Palace to explain his decision, where he told the King he found it impossible to work with the Secretary of State and questioned Rothermere's competence to be Air Minister. This got back to Lloyd-George, and Rothermere resigned.

The RNAS and the RFC merged on 1 April 1918, and David Henderson, who is alleged to have penned most of Smut's report, resigned from the Air Council and left aviation. Rothermere's replacement, Sir William Wier, persuaded Trenchard to withdraw his resignation, and on 15 June 1918 Trenchard was appointed as the General Officer Commanding the Independent Air Force (later Royal Air Force). Five months later, the First World War was over, and Churchill, as Secretary of State for War and Air, reappointed Trenchard as Chief of the Air Staff. However, Britain was in a depression and by 1921 the national debt stood at a colossal £7.8 billion. (Estimated as equivalent to £1.64 trillion at 2011 rates based on per capita GDP.) Under swathing cuts in government spending, that became known as the 'Geddes Axe', the defence budget was slashed by 42 per cent, and the RAF was facing a massive reduction in funding, equipment and personnel and a very real threat of being disbanded.

# APPENDIX H

The Lives of Key Personnel

**Samuel F. Cowdery – Showman Extraordinare**. As might be expected of a showman, there are countless myths surrounding Cody's early life, which he seemed quite happy to spread and perpetuate, and until recently a number of biographers have been taken in. A few years ago, when Mrs Jean Roberts moved into 'Pinehurst', a redbrick late-Victorian house in Farnborough, she had never heard of Samuel Cody; but one of her sons had started work at the Royal Aircraft Establishment and came home with stories of this iconic character, who had once owned their house. Jean became fascinated by the man and started to investigate his history; but the more she read, the deeper the mystery became. There was much for her to unravel. Apparently he was born in Davenport, not Birdville as the stories so fittingly claimed, he did not lose his parents when a Native American raiding party attacked their ranch, and it is unlikely he was taught to fly kites by a Chinese cook on a wagon train. He had certainly been a cattle drover and was a highly skilled horse-tamer, and it was this skill that first brought him to England. Here he met Elizabeth Mary King, daughter of the horse dealer John Blackburn Davis, although the circumstances of their meeting are another story shrouded in myth. What we do know is Elizabeth, known as Lela, was a married woman with four children and fifteen years older than Cody. An unlikely match, but they quickly discovered they were soul mates. Cody found excuses to return to England several times with his wife Maud, and they found work together with Albert Ridgeley's touring show the 'Wild West Burlesque'. This show was based on similar productions staged by William 'Buffalo Bill' Cody, who did not appreciate the competition and asked his London solicitors, Jenson, Cobb & Pearson to issue Ridgeley with a writ claiming the term 'Wild West' belonged to their client. Ridgeley conceded and closed down the show. Samuel and Maud approached Frank Albert, who was recruiting personnel for a large outdoor event he was planning at Putney in May 1891. Cody and Maud were offered work, and they began distributing fliers proclaiming themselves 'Captain Cody and Miss Cody, Buffalo Bill's son and daughter'. Inevitably, another letter arrived from Jenson, Cobb & Pearson, but Frank Albert was more defensive and refused to cooperate with their requests, saying he was not responsible for the offending leaflets, nor the organiser of the event. Cody and Maud disappeared for five months, and by the time they returned the courts had decreed 'all further proceedings in this action be stayed' and ordered William to pay Frank Albert's costs. For reasons we do not know, Maud returned to the States, where she was declared insane and admitted to an asylum where she spent the rest of her life. Within a year Samuel and Lela were appearing on stage together with their new show entitled 'Klondyke Nugget'. This was a family-based affair, with everyone helping to make costumes and scenery, and by now the couple were living as man and wife. In February 1895 their son Frank was born (he too learnt to fly and joined the Royal Flying Corps during the First World War). Samuel appears to have seen Britain initially as a place in which he could market his somewhat eccentric persona for financial gain, but as his aviation interests deepened he became more and more of an anglophile and accepted British nationality in 1909. Over the next four years he was an ever-present feature at every aviation related event in Britain; and, whilst it might perhaps be argued that his subsequent technical achievements were not outstanding, this 'larger-than-life' character was partly responsible for the adoption of a realistic attitude towards the practical uses for aviation. (Jean Roberts is now held as the world authority on the Cody family history.)

**Horatio Claude Barber** (1875-1964). Born in Croydon, Barber was one of Britain's aviation pioneers. Having purchased an aeroplane at the Salon De L'Aeronautique in Paris in 1908, he was admitted to the Aero Club of the United Kingdom in 1909 and leased a railway arch in Battersea. Along with Howard T. Wright and W.O. Manning, he formed the Aeronautical Syndicate Limited to design and produce aircraft. In September 1910, ASL took over the hangars at Hendon airfield. Barber was convinced that aircraft would have a key role in a future war, and despite inexplicably being banned from flying at Claude Grahame-White's demonstration to the Government on 12 May 1911 at Hendon, donated four Valkyries aeroplanes to the Admiralty and War Office, but there is no evidence these aircraft actually entered service. When Barber was asked to transport a box of Osram light bulbs from Shoreham to Hove, this entered the record books as the world's first cargo flight. Barber donated his fee, a princely £100, towards a prize for fellow aviators. In April 1912, ASL was sold at auction to Handley Page Ltd, and Barber gave up aeroplane manufacture to become a flying instructor at Shoreham airfield. He was the first person in Great Britain to gain an aeronautical degree. After surviving a crash, in which one of his students died, Barber tried to insure himself against any liability from passengers he carried in his aircraft. This was unknown at the time and so Lloyd asked him to write the first aviation third-party insurance policy. Barber was commissioned as a Probationary Second Lieutenant in the RFC in October 1914 and rose to the rank of Captain during the First World War. After the war he served in the Royal Air Force, continued his involvement in aircraft insurance and was in charge of all flying training in England. Barber published two books, *The Aeroplane Speaks* in 1917 and *Aerobatics* in 1927. He lived in Amesbury until his death on 6 July 1964.

**George Bertram Cockburn** (1872-1931). George Bertram Cockburn OBE was born on 8 January 1872 in Birkenhead on the Wirral. The first child of George Cockburn and his second wife Katherine Jessie Stitt (née Bertram), he had two half brothers and a sister from his parent's previous marriages. A family with Scottish roots, Cockburn attended Loretto School in Musselburgh from 1887 until 1892, when he went to Oxford to read Natural Sciences specialising in Chemistry. He graduated from New College in 1895 and found work as a research chemist as St George's Hospital in London. When his father died in 1901, Cockburn returned to the family home in Birkenhead and lived with his mother and his unmarried sister, Mary. When Katherine died in 1903, George and Mary sold the house and moved to Gloucestershire. At some point around this time, it is noted that Cockburn was a keen rugby player, and apparently selected to represent Scotland, although his rugby-playing career is not well documented.

By February 1909, Cockburn had become interested in aeronautics and was elected a member of the Aeronautical Club of the United Kingdom, and later that year became the first pupil in Henri Farman's flying school based in Châlons-sur-Marne. There, he flew for the first time in June 1909, and that summer took part in the *Le Grande Semaine D'Aviation de la Champagne* at Rheims. He was the sole British entrant in the premier event of the air meet, the Gordon Bennett Cup, on 29 August, but ignominiously was the only competitor not to finish after he collided with a haystack. On 26 April 1910 Cockburn was awarded Royal Aero Club Certificate No.5, and moved into a house in the village of St Mary Bourne, near Andover, and made arrangements to base a Farman III biplane, which he had brought back from France, at Lark Hill, where he struck up a lasting friendship with John Fulton.

That summer, Cockburn entered a flying competition in Wolverhampton and won a £100 prize, but following the death of Charles Rolls at Bournemouth in July, Cockburn did not fly competitively again; although he did continue to promote air races as an incentive to aircraft development. Rolls was supposed to have started teaching British officers to fly, and when his replacement, Cyril Grace, was also drowned following a flying accident, the War Office asked Cockburn to accept the task. Disappointed with the progress he had seen the French military were making in teaching their officers to fly, he agreed and said he would do so free of charge. Among his first pupils were the first four naval officers selected by the Admiralty to under go flying training at Eastchurch. Cockburn was appointed an observer for the RAeC Committee and oversaw many of the flying tests taken at Lark Hill.

In 1912, Cockburn became a founding member of the RAeC's Public Safety & Accidents Investigation Committee. The following year he resigned his Fellowship of the Chemical Society, and with war approaching was appointed Inspector of Aeroplanes for the Royal Flying Corps. In February 1913 he married Lilian Woodhouse, and their daughter Joan was born in 1914. Cockburn was awarded his OBE in the New Year Honours of 1918 for his services to aviation, and shortly afterwards became head of the newly established Accidents Branch of the Department of the Controller-General of Civil Aviation at the Air Ministry. He died on 25 February 1931, aged fifty-nine, at Larksborough, near Whitchurch.

**Robert Loraine MC DSO** (1876-1935). Running away from school at the age of thirteen to follow his parents into the theatre, against their wishes, Loraine worked with a touring repertory company for five years before getting his first London role. He married fellow actor Julie Opp, but three years later they were divorced, and shortly afterwards he volunteered to serve with the Montgomeryshire Yeomanry in the Boer War, where he was twice mentioned in dispatches. He returned to acting and was most successful in Shaw's *Man and Superman*. In 1909, having witnessed Blériot's first channel crossing, he decided to buy an aeroplane and travelled to Pau to learn to fly (in his diaries he uses the term 'joystick', possibly the first recorded use of this phrase), and moved onto Henri Farman's school at Mourmelons where he obtained his ACF Certificate on 21 June 1910 (under the alias Robert Jones). Whilst in France, Loraine purchased a Farman biplane and met Jules Védrines, who he employed as his engineer and chauffeur. During the Bournemouth Aviation week, Loraine became the first pilot to fly in a rainstorm and was forced to fly across The Solent to the Isle of Wight, which gave him the idea to attempt the first flight over to Ireland. On 11 September he departed from Holyhead, climbed to an altitude of 4,000ft and using a compass strapped to his right knee, set course for Ireland. It was fortunate that Loraine had chosen to climb so high for the transit, as on four separate occasions his engine stopped. But as he dived towards the sea, Loraine was able to restart the engine and continue the flight. The engine stopped for a fifth and final time, just short of the Irish coast. Unable to get it started he abandoned the machine and swam the short distance to the shore.

Despite his soggy conclusion, the 52-mile crossing was lauded a success and Loraine returned to London to open in a play entitled *The Man From The Sea*. For the crossing and other aviation achievements, the RAeC subsequently awarded Loraine a Silver Medal. He entered the *Daily Mail* Circuit of Britain race in 1911, but could not compete, although his assistant Védrines finished in second place. At the outbreak of the First World War, Loraine joined the RFC as a 2nd Lieutenant in the Special Reserve, but after two crashes was assigned not as a pilot but as an observer. Whilst posted to No.3 Squadron, he was wounded, and after his recovery returned to France as a pilot. In October 1915 he was awarded the Military Cross for shooting down an enemy Albatros, described in the citation as a feat of conspicuous gallantry and skill. In March 1916, he took command of No.40 Squadron at Gosport, but was not a popular CO owing to the high standards he set. This did not hold him back, and the following year he became CO of No.14 Wing at Andover as a Lieutenant Colonel (although later reverted to Major in somewhat suspicious circumstances after being acquitted of being drunk on duty at court martial). He returned to flying duty in France as CO 211 Squadron, but was wounded a second time and returned home, where he began acting again. He died in London on 23 December 1935.

# APPENDIX I

## Who was the First British Pilot?

The problem with identifying who was the first British pilot stems from the simple fact that in the early years you did not have to have a license to fly; the very first pilots were self taught, and many British pilots like Dickson, Cockburn and Fulton had obtained an Aéro-Club de France (ACF) certificate. As we have seen, the first person to fly a powered aeroplane in Britain was Samuel Cody, but he did not become a British citizen until 1909, so his achievement must be logged up to an American. It is a matter of some controversy, who was the first Englishman to repeat that feat. The honour was given to John T.C. Moore-Brabazon. His first flight in Britain was completed at the Isle of Sheppey on 2 May 1909; however, supporters of Alliott V. Roe knew he had been experimenting at Brooklands, and claimed that Roe had flown from the racetrack on 8 June 1908 (some months before even Cody's first flight). Roe, however, accepted the attempt was un-witnessed and, in the knowledge he had only covered of about 60 yards at a height of no more than 2–3ft, felt he had no claim to the title. But the argument would not go away and the Royal Aero Club Committee stepped-in to resolve the dispute. They decided in favour of Brabazon, who it should be said enjoyed close links with the Aero Club, whilst Roe incurred the displeasure of Brookland's owners, who felt he had accomplished something illegal and immoral. Brabazon was awarded Royal Aeronautical Club Certificate (RAeCC) No.1 on 8 March 1910, and the Hon. Charles Rolls was given certificate No.2 the same day. Rolls had actually been taught to fly before Brabazon and awarded ACF certificate No. 23 on 6 Jan 1910; as had Mr Mortimer Singer (ACF No.24) and Claude Graham-White (ACF No.30). Brabazon did not receive his ACF certificate (No.40) until 8 March 1910. However, the first four British certificates were allocated by the Royal Aero Club in alphabetical order.

Claude Grahame-White had enrolled at the Blériot factory at Neuilly-sur-Seine in 1909, whilst waiting for the Blériot XII he had ordered to be completed, and received his ACF certificate (No.30) on 4 January 1910, and was, therefore, the first licensed British pilot. George B. Cockburn was the first pilot to be trained at the Henri Farman School in June 1909, but did not receive an ACF certificate; he was awarded RAeCC No.5 on the basis of his accomplishments in France, in April 1910. Samuel Cody was given certificate No.10 on 7 June 1910. That same month, Robert Loraine was learning to fly in France under the pseudonym 'Robert Jones', whilst Horatio Barber did not qualify for his RAeCC until after his move to Hendon, by which time he had built a number of different aeroplanes.

Early military pilots learnt to fly of their own volition. Bertram Dickson obtained his ACF certificate on 13 May 1910 whilst still serving, but never obtained a RAeC certificate. Having also been taught in France, Lancelot Gibbs received RAeC certificate No.10, but was a member of the reserves. Capt. John Fulton was trained at Bristol Flying School at Lark Hill where he received RAeC certificate No.27 on 15 November 1910, and was, therefore, the first person serving in the regular Army or Navy to qualify; but Lieut Reginald Cammell was the first military pilot to fly on duty. Although he had flown in France that summer, and subsequently at Lark Hill he did not receive RAeC certificate No.45 until 31 December. Cammell was the first military pilot to hold balloon, airship and aeroplane pilot certificates, and one of only three pilots ever to achieve this. The first Naval pilot was Lieut G.C. Colmore RN, who gained RAeC certificate No.15 at his own expense on 21 June 1910. Lieuts Charles Samson and Arthur Longmore RN were trained by Cockburn at Eastchurch, and were awarded their RAeC certificates on 25 April 1911 (Lieut Wilfred Parke RN, who had paid for his training at Brooklands, received his that same day). The first British woman to obtain her RAeC certificate was Mrs Hilda Hewlett who qualified on 29 August 1911, although Miss Edith Maud Cook (aka Spencer 'Viola' Kavanagh) had flown solo in Blériots at Grahame-White's school at Pau early in 1910, before becoming a professional parachute jumper; she died making a jump in July 1910. Hilda Hewlett's husband was also a qualified pilot, and upon receiving her certificate she spent time teaching her son how to fly before he joined the Royal Naval Air Service.

# BIBLIOGRAPHY AND FURTHER RECOMMENDED READING

Some of these publications have provided quotations; others give background reading. By the nature of the subject and its recorded history, no guarantee of accuracy of any individual publication is offered. (Sources are listed by author in alphabetic then date order.)

Barnes, C.H., *Bristol Aircraft Since 1910*, Putnam, 1964

Beaumont, André, *Mes Trois Grandes Courses*, 1912

Berryman, David, *Wiltshire Airfields of the Second World War*, Countryside Books, 2009

Boyle, Andrew, *Trenchard: Man of Vision*, 1962

Brett, Dallas, *The History of British Aviation 1908-1914*, John Hamilton Ltd., 1932

Broke-Smith, P.W.L., *History of Early British Military Aeronautics*, Cedric Chivers Ltd., 1952

Bruce, Gordon, *C.S. Rolls: Pioneer Aviator*, Monmouth District Museum Service, 1978

Bruce, J.M., *Aeroplanes of the Royal Flying Corps (Military Wing)*, Putnam, 1982

——— 'A Pointless Exercise', *Aeroplane Monthly*, March–April 1998

Butcher, P.E., *Skill and Devotion: A personal reminiscence of the famous No. 2 Squadron Royal Flying Corps*, Radio Modeller Book Division, 1971

Churchill, Winston, *The World Crisis 1911-1918*, Thornton Butterworth Ltd., 1931

Croydon CBE RAF (Retd), Air Cdre Bill, *Early Birds: A Short History of How Flight came to Sheppey*, Publicity Matters, 2006

Draper, Major Chris, *The Mad Major*, The Aire Review Ltd, 1962

Driver, High, *The Birth of Military Aviation 1903-1914*, Woodbridge & Rochester, 1997

Dunn, Michael J., *The Air Battalion Royal Engineers*, Cross & Cockdale International Journal Vol. 42 No. 2, 2012

——— *James Templer and the Birth of British Military Aviation*, Cross & Cockdale International Journal Vol. 43 No. 2, 2012

Frater, Alexander, *The Balloon Factory: The Story of the Men who Built Britain's First Flying Machines*, Picador, 2008

Gollin, Alfred, *No Longer an Island: Britain and the Wright Brothers*, Stanfrod University Press, 1984

—— *The Impact of Air Power on the British People and their Government*, Stanford University Press, 1989

Goodall, Michael H. and Albert F. Tagg, *British Aircraft Before the Great War*, Schiffer Aviation Books, 2001

Grahame-White, Claude and Harry Harper, *The Aeroplane (Romance of Reality Series)*, T.C. & E.C. Jack Ltd, 1914

Grayer, Jeffrey, *Rails Across the Plain: The Amesbury – Bulford Railway*, Noodle Books, 2011

Hall, Malcolm, *From Balloon to Boxkite: The Royal Engineers & Early British Aeronautics*, Amberley Publishing Ltd, 2010

Hare, Paul, *The Royal Aircraft Factory*, Putnam, 1990

Harper, Harry, *Man's Conquest of the Air*, The Scientific Book Club, 1942

—— *Ace Air Reporter*, The Scientific Book Club, 1944

—— *My Fifty Years in Flying*, Associated Newspapers Ltd, 1956

Howard, Fred, *Wilbur and Orville: The Story of the Wright Brothers*, Robert Hale, 1987

Jackson, Robert, *Strike From The Sea*, Arthur Barket Ltd, 1970

James, N.D.G., *Gunners at Larkhill*, Gresham Books Ltd, 1984

—— *Plain Soldiering: A History of the Armed Forces on Salisbury Plain*, Hobnob Press, 1987

Jarrett, Philip, *Frank MacClean: Godfather to British Naval Aviation*, Pen & Sword, 2011

Jones, H.A., *Per Ardua ad Astra: Sir David Henderson KCB KCVO DSO – A Memoir*, 1931

Kelly, Fred C. ed., *Miracle at Kitty Hawk (the Letters of Wilbur & Orville Wright)*, Farrar, Straus & Giroux Ltd, reprinted By Da Capo Press, 2002

King, Brad, *The Royal Naval Air Service 1912-1918,* Hikoki, 1997

Kipling, Rudyard, *The New Army in Training*, Macmillan, 1915

Lewis, Bruce, *A Few of the First: Thirteen first-hand accounts of flying in the RFC and RNAS during the First World War*, Pen & Sword, 1997

Lewis, Peter, *Squadron Histories RFC, RNAS and RAF 1912-1959*, Putnam, 1959

Long, Jack T.C., *Three's Company: An Illustrated History of No.3 (Fighter) Squadron RAF*, Pen & Sword, 2005

Loraine, Winifred, *Robert Loraine Actor Soldier Airman*, Collins, 1938

Munro, R.L., *The Flying Shadow*, an unpublished autobiography of Capt. Dickson dated 1994, held by the Museum of Army Aviation

—— *The Royal Flying Corps: A History*, Muller, 1965

Parker, Norman, *Army Airfield No.3 Larkhill – Where it All Began*, Army air Corps Journal No.10, 1984

Pembrey, Malcolm, *Colonel James Templar and the Birth of Aviation at Farnborough*, Royal Aeronautical Society (Farnborough Branch), revised 2007

Penrose, Harald, *British Aviation – The Pioneer Years 1903-1914*, Putnam, 1967

Priddle, Ron, *Wings Over Wiltshire*, ALD Design & Print, 2003

Raleigh, Sir Walter A., *War in the Air Vol. 1*, Oxford University Press, 1922

Reese, Peter, *The Flying Cowboy: The Story of Samuel F Cody, Britain's First Airman*, Tempus Publishing, 2006

Sanger, Ray, *Blériot in Britain 1899-1927*, Air Britain Publications, 2008

Sykes, Maj. Gen. Sir F.H., *Aviation in War and Peace*, 1921

Treadwell, Terry and Wood, Alan, *The Royal Naval Air Service*, Tempus Publishing, 1999

Turner, Charles C., *The Old Flying Days*, Samson Low, 1927

Walker, Percy B., *Early Aviation at Farnborough: The History of the Royal Aircraft Establishment Vols. I & II*, MacDonald, 1971

White, George, *Tramlines to the Stars: George White of Bristol*, Redcille Press Ltd, 1995

Wells, H.G., *The War in the Air*, Pall Mall Magazine, 1908

Wright, Peter, *Larkhill: The Army and the Air*, Cross & Cockdale International Journal Vol.31 No.4, 2000

Serano, Henry, *Contact: The Story of the Early Aviators*, Dover Publications, 2002

Unknown, *Early Flying Machines*, Thomas Nelson & Sons, 1909

Hansard from 1911-1912. Various issues of *Flight* magazine, particularly the 'From the British Flying Grounds' articles published therein between 1910-14, *Aero* magazine and Cross & Cockade Journal, including individual editions listed above, contemporary newspapers and journals, The Bristol Reference Library. Air Cdre. W.H. Croydon for access to his article: 'Dunne – the Designer of the Modern Aeroplane'. Norman Parker and the Amesbury Aviation Heritage Centre; Mrs Jean Baker. The National Archive. The Bruce/Leslie collection of photographs held by the Fleet Air Arm Museum, and the extensive photography archive of Jimmy Fuller Amesbury. Period maps are reproduced with kind permission of the Ordnance Survey.

Websites include: http://1914-1918.Invasionzone.com (The Great War Forum); www.armyflying.com; www.bac2010.co.uk; www.flightglobal.com; www.london-gazette.co.uk; http://sfcody.org.uk; www.bbc.co.uk; www.british-history.ac.uk; www.rafmuseum.org.uk; www.this-is-amesbury.co.uk; www.heritage-print.com; www.earlyaviators.com; www.gracesguide.co.uk. A third-party FOI request to the Office for Public Sector Information in 2005 requested clarification on copyright restrictions. Their Information Policy Adviser said, Crown copyright protection in published material lasts for fifty years from the end of the year in which the material was first published and after that point it may be used freely. Credits for holding sources of such material are given where possible.

# NOTES

Introduction

1   The War Office: Staff headquarters for the British Army
2   Warminster Journal, 1909
3   Imperial War Museum. Chanute had experimented with gliders himself, with some success, and the Wright Brothers based the design of their own Flyer on his most successful aircraft.
5   Letter quoted in *Wilbur & Orville: The Story of the Wright Brothers* by Fred Howard (1987)

Chapter 1

1   Telegram, 17 Dec 1903, quoted in *Miracle at Kitty Hawk* edited by Fred C. Kelly (1996)
2   Quoted in History of World War 1
3   The founder of the Avro Aeroplane Company.
4   The Times Engineering Supplement, 1906
5   Lt Col J.E Capper CB RE to RUSI 1906, quoted in *The Old Flying Days* by Charles Turner (1927)
6   *Wilbur & Orville: The Story of the Wright Brothers* by Fred Howard (1987)
7   Wilbur Wright's letter to John Capper, quoted in *Miracle at Kitty Hawk* edited by Fred C. Kelly (1996)
8   Wilbur Wright's letter to Congressman Robert Nevin dated 18 Jan 1905, quoted in *Miracle at Kitty Hawk* edited by Fred C. Kelly (1996)
9   Wilbur Wright's letter to Octavus Chanute dated 1 Jun 1905, quoted in *Miracle at Kitty Hawk* edited by Fred C. Kelly (1996)
10  War Office to Capper, quoted in *No Longer an Island* by Alfred M. Gollin (1984)
11  Capper's report to the War Office, quoted in *No Longer an Island* by Alfred M. Gollin (1984)

Chapter 2

1   Capper's report to the Royal Engineer Committee, quoted in No Longer an Island by Alfred M. Gollin (1984)
2   Courtesy of Jean Roberts (www.sfcody.org.uk)
3   Cody to the War Office, 1901, courtesy of Jean Roberts and the BBC.
4   Cody had asked the Admiralty for £25,000, plus a salary of £1250 per annum, six weeks holiday and a further £25,000 on completion of his work.
5   Capper's letter to the War Office, 3 Jun 1904, quoted in *Early Aviation at Farnborough*, Vol. 1, by Percy Walker (1971)
6   Samuel Cody acquired the nickname 'Colonel' from his audiences who mistook him for 'Buffalo Bill'. He was very conscious of the effect it had on his army colleagues but

'lightheartedly' adopted it after the Military Aircraft Trial when he was addressed as such by HRH King George V.

7    *Pearson's Magazine*, July 1906, courtesy of RAF Museum, Hendon.

8    In America between 2003-2009 at least four replicas of the Wright Flyer crashed in attempts to replicate the first flight.

9    Courtesy of Air Cdre Bill Croydon CBE RAF (Retd)

10   Capper writing to Dunne, 6 June 1906 (Air 1/1613/204/88/17)

11   Capper writing to the Master General of the Ordnance (1906), quoted in *No Longer an Island* by Alfred M. Gollin (1984)

12   Equivalent to 52.5p and worth approximately £30 at 2012 rates, Dunne was getting about half of what Cody was being paid.

13   The Atholl Highlanders were formed in 1777 to fight alongside the British Army in the North American colonies, were reformed prior to the visit by Queen Victoria in 1839 and she presented them with regimental colours in 1844. Although the regiment has never seen active service, many of its men served in the Yeomanry with The Scottish Horse in both world wars. The 10th Duke reformed the regiment in 1966 as a ceremonial bodyguard, and today it remains the last private army in Europe.

14   Col Capper's report to the Director of Ordnance, quoted in 'Early Aviation at Farnborough', Vol.2 by Percy B. Walker

15   *British Aviation: The Pioneer Years* by Harald Penrose

16   Lord Esher's report to the Committee for Imperial Defence, quoted in 'Early Aviation at Farnborough', Vol.2 by Percy B. Walker

17   Richard Fairey would go onto join Short Brothers as Chief Engineer before forming his own company, Fairey Aviation, in 1915.

Chapter 3

1    *Flight* magazine, 6 February 1909, p.77

2    'The War in the Air', Vol. 1, by Walter Raleigh (1922)

3    Conversation with Norman Parker, 2011.

4    When ASL departed Lark Hill for Hendon in Sept 1910 Bannister remained, working for Capt. John Fulton and was then employed by BCAC.

5    *Flight* magazine, 12 March 1910, p.184

6    Conversation with Norman Parker, 2011

7    Charles Gray, editor *The Aero*, 1910

8    *Flight* magazine 1910

9    *The Old Flying Days* by Charles Turner (1927), p.243

10   Monmouth District Museum Service

11   *The Flying Shadow* by R.L. Munro (unpublished)

12   Widdows letter to Lord Northcliffe, 15 September 1909, quoted in T*he Impact of Air Power on the British People* by Alfred M. Gollin (1989)

13   'The Early Days of Flying', an essay by Maj. Eugene Gerrard, courtesy of Mark Barber

Chapter 4

1    Sir George White's speech 1910, quoted in *Flight* magazine, 15 February 1940, p.149.

2    Sir George formed four companies that day, including the Bristol Aeroplane Co. Ltd. Although a very loyal Bristolian, he thought British & Colonial a better brand for dealing on an international aviation market. Short Bros are now widely acknowledged as the first British aeroplane manufacturer, and Handley Page was launched ahead of Sir George's companies; but by scale of the operation, BCAC was significantly larger than these garagista-type operations, and can therefore justifiably claim its place alongside them at the start of the British aviation industry.

3    Charles Grey, writing in *The Aero*, February 1911, quoted in *Tramlines to the Stars* by George White (1995)
4    Aero engines were costly and presented at least 50 per cent of the total cost of an aeroplane. Buying another would have been an expensive option.
5    Some sources give the date of this flight as 29 July 1910
6    '...And Bristol Fashion' *Flight* magazine 2 March 1939

Chapter 5
1    First published in *Boys Own Paper*, 13 January 1912
2    Origin: French – gliding flight
3    *The Flying Shadow* by R.L. Munro (unpublished)
4    Harry Harper writing in *Flight* magazine, 15 February 1952
5    The Pathé footage is viewable on-line at www.britishpathe.com
6    *Flight*, 27 September 1910
7    *British Aviation: The Pioneer Years* by Harald Penrose (1967)
8    *British Aviation: The Pioneer Years* by Harald Penrose (1967)
9    *The Flying Shadow* by R.L. Munro (unpublished)
10   *My Fifty Years in Flying* by Harry Harper (1956)
11   *The Flying Shadow* by R.L. Munro (unpublished)
12   *Flight* magazine, 1 October 1910, p.803
13   *The Flying Shadow* by R.L. Munro (unpublished)
14   *The Daily Mirror*, 22 September 1910
15   *My Fifty Years in Flying* by Harry Harper (1956)
16   *British Aviation: The Pioneer Years* by Harald Penrose (1967)
17   *Birmingham Gazette*, 22 September 1910
18   *The Flying Shadow* by R.L. Munro (unpublished)
19   *The Daily Mirror*, 22 September 1910
20   Arthur Edwards was subsequently recruited by Bristol Engine Company and worked as the Apprentice Supervisor at Filton.
21   'British Aviation: The Pioneer Years' by Harald Penrose (1967)
22   *The Daily Mirror*, 21 September 1910
23   *The Daily Mail*, 23 September 1910
24   Varying accounts of the date when Loraine first got involved in these flights are available; some suggesting his presence was always intended, others, such as Harry Harper in his report for the *Daily Mail*, that only two pilots flew on 21 September 1910; whereas Holt-Thomas later stated, 'Dickson was the only pilot'. There is a suggestion that Loraine flew his own aeroplane, but to have conducted the radio trial described later, he must been flying a Bristol machine on that occasion. Whatever the facts, this uncertainty does little to affect the historical significance of these flights. Quoted in 'British Notes of the Week', *Flight* magazine, 1 October 1910, p.802
25   'British Notes of the Week', *Flight* magazine, 1 October 1910, p.802
26   The monument and surrounding land did not come into public ownership until 1918.

Chapter 6
1    *Cross & Cockade*, Vol. 31, No. 4 (2000), p.207

Chapter 7
1    Boothby was attached to the Balloon School, had no more aeroplane experience than Cammell.
2    Rex Cammell quoted in *From Balloon to Boxkite* by Malcolm Hall (2010)
3    Rex Cammell letter to Col Capper quoted in *From Balloon to Boxkite* by Malcolm Hall (2010)

4    Rex Cammell quoted in *From Balloon to Boxkite* by Malcolm Hall (2010)
5    Rex Cammell letter to Col Capper quoted in *From Balloon to Boxkite* by Malcolm Hall (2010)
6    Rex Cammell letter to Col Capper quoted in *From Balloon to Boxkite* by Malcolm Hall (2010)
7    Rex Cammell letter to Col Capper quoted in *From Balloon to Boxkite* by Malcolm Hall (2010)
8    Col Capper to Rex Cammell quoted in *From Balloon to Boxkite* by Malcolm Hall (2010)
9    Rex Cammell quoted in *From Balloon to Boxkite* by Malcolm Hall (2010)
10   Rex Cammell quoted in *From Balloon to Boxkite* by Malcolm Hall (2010)
11   Charles Gray writing in *The Aero*, 4 January 1911, quoted in *The Aeroplanes of the Royal Flying Corps* (Military Wing) by J.M. Bruce
12   The Balloon Factory, and later Royal Aircraft Factory, were forbidden from building aeroplanes, to avoid accusations that the government was competing with private constructors, but by the subterfuge of 'rebuilding' were apparently able to circumvent this restriction.
13   SE.1 in this instance stood for Santos Experimental No.1, not to be confused with the later aeroplanes the Royal Aircraft Factory would produce.
14   *Flight* magazine, 26 August 1911, p.741
15   'From the British Flying Grounds', *Flight* magazine, 7 January 1911
16   'From the British Flying Grounds', *Flight* magazine, 7 January 1911

Chapter 8
1    *The Old Flying Days* by Charles Turner (1927)
2    *The Old Flying Days* by Charles Turner (1927)
3    *The Old Flying Days* by Charles Turner (1927)
4    *The Old Flying Days* by Charles Turner (1927)
5    *The Old Flying Days* by Charles Turner (1927)
6    Conversation with Sir George White (2010), courtesy of Ted Mustard
7    Eric Furlong's account, quoted in *A Few of the First* by Bruce Lewis (1997)
8    *The Mad Major* by Maj. C. Draper DSC (1962)
9    *History of Early English Military Aeronautics* by P.W.L. Broke-Smith, *Royal Engineers Journal* (1952)
10   *Windy Days* by Charles Turner, quoted in *Flight* magazine, 2 January 1941

Chapter 9
1    Lord Esher's note on Aerial Navigation, dated 4 October 1910 (AIR/1/2311/221/32)
2    'The Army & Aeronautics – The New Air Battalion', *Flight* magazine, 4 March 1911, p.179
3    The Royal Engineers had been involved in aeronautics, with balloons, since 1870.
4    'The Army & Aeronautics – The New Air Battalion', *Flight* magazine, 4 March 1911, p.179
5    Training for the RAeCC cost £75, a not inconsiderable sum of money in 1911 (equating to about £6000 and rather similar to fees being quoted for PPL (Private Pilot License) training today)
6    Seely to Rothschild Hansard, 1911, Vol. 23 (CC1981–1982)
7    Seely to Sandys Hansard, 1911, Vol. 24 (214–215)
8    Capt. Edward Maitland Royal Essex was a balloonist, returned to this skill after an accident at Lark Hill and was seconded to the Air Battalion on 19 August 1911 in the spring of 1911. He became CO No.1 'The Gas Company' and carried out the first ever parachute descent from an airship in 1913.

9    'From the British Flying Grounds', *Flight* magazine, 20 May 1911, p.446

10   Retold by Michael J. Dunne in *Cross & Cockade International*, Autumn 2011

Chapter 10

1    A full list of Circuit of Britain competitors is at Appendix B.

2    Quoted from a report in *The Times* in *The Flying Cathedral* by Arthur Gould-Lee (1965)

3    Quoted from a report in *The Times* in *The Flying Cathedral* by Arthur Gould-Lee (1965)

4    *Mes Trois Grand Course (My Three Great Races)* by André Beaumont, 1912

5    'From the British Flying Grounds', *Flight* magazine, 5 August 1911, p.682

6    'The Great Race' Editorial, *Flight* magazine, 5 August 1911, p.670

7    Frank McClean quoted in 'Frank McClean: Godfather to British Naval Aviation' by Peter Jarrett (2011)

Chapter 11

1    No original Bristol Boxkites survive today, although three authentic reproductions were created for the film *Those Magnificent Men in Their Flying Machines* (Dir. Ken Annakin 1965) – thought to have been inspired by the Circuit of Britain Air Race. On completion, one of the Boxkites was sent to Australia, one to the Bristol City Museum and Art Gallery, and the only remaining airworthy machine given to the Shuttleworth Collection in Bedfordshire, which is still flown during their flying displays whenever the weather permits.

2    Bannerman's memo to the Dir. of Fortification & Works, dated 8 September 1911, quoted by Michael J. Dunne in *Cross & Cockade International*, Autumn 2011

3    'From the British Flying Grounds', *Flight* magazine, 8 July 1911, p.592

Chapter 12

1    Bannerman's letter to the Chief Engineer of Aldershot Command (AIR/1/1608/204/85/30)

2    *Flight* magazine, quoted in 'The History of British Aviation' by Dallas Brett (1933)

3    *Flight* magazine, quoted in 'The History of British Aviation' by Dallas Brett (1933)

4    *The Royal Flying Corps: A History*, by Geoffrey Norris, 1965

5    *From Balloons to Boxkites* by Malcolm Hall (2010)

6    Brakes on aeroplanes were still the exception, pilots having to rely on the drag of their tailskid, an up-hill slope or some other means to bring themselves to a halt. From 'Air Eddies', *Flight* magazine, 9 September 1911, p.788

7    (Air/1/737/737/204/2/6) No. 3 Sqn RFC Weekly Training Reports. Reproduced by *Cross & Cockade* Autumn 2011

Chapter 13

1    Speech reported in *The Times*, 22 July 1911

2    'Aircraft for use in War' by Maj. Bannerman in *Journal of the Royal Artillery* (1911), p.185

3    Hansard, Vol. 28 (860–861), 18 July 1911

4    Manufacturers had yet to devise a standard system of aircraft controls, and those fitted to the Valkyrie were quite different from the system used by Blériot, which Cammell was familiar with.

5    Obituary printed in *Flight* magazine, 23 September 1911, p.830

6    Hansard, Vol. 30 (cc659–677)

7    The Air Battalion had been renamed No.1 Aeroplane Section Royal Engineers in Sept 1911, but this name appears to have been rarely used.

8    Cockburn, quoted in 'Aircraft of the Royal Flying Corps (Military Wing)' by J.M. Bruce (1982)

9 'The Government and the Aeroplane Industry', *Flight* magazine, 9 December 1911, p.1069
10 Four years later, the deputation of British aircraft manufacturers formed the Society of British Aircraft Constructors (SBAC)
11 *Pall Mall Gazette*, 18 January 1912, quoted in *Flight* magazine editorial, 27 January 1912

Chapter 14
1 *Daily Mail*, Nov 1906, the day after Santos Dumont made the first powered flight in Europe
2 *The War in the Air*, Vol. 1 by Walter Raleigh (1922)
3 Charles Grey writing in *The Aeroplane* in 1911, quoted by Michael Dunne in *Cross & Cockade*, Winter 2011
4 Fulton's letter to Seely, Admiralty Record Office, Case 5762 ADM273/2
5 Minute by Churchill dated 9 December 1911, ADM 116/1278, quoted in *The Birth of Military Aviation* by Hugh Driver (1997)
6 Qualifying at Brooklands under the name Henry Davidson in August 1911 Henderson was, at the age of 49, the oldest person in Britain to have qualified as a pilot at that time.
7 Capt Dickson's statement to the Technical Sub-Committee, National Archives
8 *Flight* magazine, 16 November 1912, p.1046

Chapter 15
1 Capt. Paine RN earned his nickname for profane language 'the effect of which on young Army officers who deviated from RFC discipline could be most salutary.'
2 'From Sea to Sky' by Sir Arthur Longmore (1946)
3 RFC Terms of Enlistment, reproduced in *Flight* magazine, 8 June 1912, p.510
4 'The Mad Major' by Maj. Christopher Draper DSC (1962)

Chapter 16
1 All quotes in this section are from the Coroner's Inquest into the death of Leonard Williams, dated 24 May 1912 (reproduced from http://salisburyinquests.wordpress.com)
2 'The Catastrophe on Salisbury Plain', *Flight* magazine 13 July 1912, p.634
3 The Airmans' Cross memorial was removed by English Heritage in 2012 and relocated within the perimeter of the Stonehenge Visitors Centre, although the new position still does not mark the exact crash location, it is now thought to be closer to the probable site than it was originally (there is no official record of the site but an investigation in July 2012, before work on the visitor centre commenced, identified the site with some certainty).

Chapter 17
1 Hansard, Vol. 30 (cc659–70), 30 October 1911
2 Hansard, Vol. 30 (cc659–70), 30 October 1911
3 *Flight* magazine, 29 June 1912
4 The validity of Cody's patents had been questioned by the War Office from the outset, on the basis of a report suggesting his work was not an original invention, and therefore the patent offered the Government no protection from production of similar machines.
5 Sources differ on the number of sheds, with some claiming as many as twenty-two were constructed. It is not certain whether these structures were the familiar double-bay sheds similar to those the company had previously erected at Lark Hill, or whether the larger number included other buildings already on site. I feel this is likely to be the case, with some competitors using No.3 Squadrons sheds as they had moved over to Upavon for the duration, and BCAC already had their own buildings on site.

6    'The Military Aeroplane Competition', *Flight* magazine 3 August 1912, p.693

7    *Flight* magazine, 3 August 1912, p.696

8    'Military Aeroplane Trials and Some Side Issues', *Flight* magazine, 31 August 1912

9    *Three's Company* by J.T.C. Long (2005)

10   Cody, quoted in *The Flying Cowboy* by Peter Reese (2006)

11   'Military Aeroplane Trials and Some Side Issues', *Flight* magazine, 31 August 1912, p.793

12   Charlie Tye's recollections, quoted in *A Few of the First* by Bruce Lewis (1997)

13   S.T. Swaby's letter to *Flight* magazine, 24 August 1912, p.782

14   *The History of British Aviation 1909–14* by Dallas Brett (*c*.1933)

15   *The History of British Aviation 1909–14* by Dallas Brett (*c*.1933)

16   *The History of British Aviation 1909–14* by Dallas Brett (*c*.1933)


Chapter 18

1    'Parke's Dive', *Flight* magazine, 31 August 1912, p.787


Chapter 19

1    'British Notes of the Week', *Flight* magazine, 21 September 1912, p.859


Chapter 20

1    Churchill, as First Lord of the Admiralty, did not repeat the edict and Naval crews continued to fly monoplanes; however, the consequences of a protracted, and possibly extended ban on monoplane operation worried the manufacturers.


Chapter 21

1    Correspondence from the RAF Museum Hendon

2    Correspondence from the RAF Museum Hendon

3    'From the British Flying Grounds', *Flight* magazine, 28 March 1914, p.345

4    In 1911, two years before Cholmondley's flight, Jullerot was regularly landing at Lark Hill after dark, simply by the light of a bonfire lit on the airfield (see *Flight*, 9 September 1911) and there are many similar accounts of landings after sunset.

5    Henri Jullerot, quoted in *Wings Over Wiltshire* by Rod Priddle (2003)

6    *Bristol Aircraft Since 1910* by Chris Barnes (1964), p.91


Chapter 22

1    The sinister overtones of this phrase today meant nothing to the pre-First World War population.

2    *Flight* magazine Editorial, 1914

3    War Office letter to Sykes, quoted in *Flight* magazine, 10 July 1914, p.741


Chapter 23

1    Quoted in *A Few of the First* by Bruce Lewis (1997)

2    *London Gazette*, 2 April 1918


Chapter 24

1    *Rails Across the Plain* by Jeffrey Grayer


Chapter 25

1    Aerial Navigation Order made by the Secretary of State, dated 2 Aug 1914, under the Aerial Navigation Acts 1911 and 1913

2    *The New Army in Training* by Rudyard Kipling (1914), p.38

3    *Dairy of a Night Bomber Pilot* by Clive Semple

# INDEX

Note: military ranks shown here are those applicable at the time of this account and may not reflect higher ranks obtained in an individual's career.